# The Boer War

# MILESTONES
## IN MODERN
## WORLD HISTORY

The Boer War

The Bolshevik
Revolution

The British
Industrial Revolution

The Chinese
Cultural Revolution

The Collapse of
the Soviet Union

The Congress of Vienna

The Cuban Revolution

D-Day and the
Liberation of France

The End of Apartheid
in South Africa

The Establishment
of the State of Israel

The French Revolution
and the Rise
of Napoleon

The Great Irish Famine

The Indian
Independence
Act of 1947

The Iranian Revolution

The Manhattan Project

The Marshall Plan

The Mexican
Revolution

The Treaty of Nanking

The Treaty of Versailles

The Universal
Declaration of
Human Rights

# MILESTONES
## IN MODERN
## WORLD HISTORY

# The Boer War

## LOUISE CHIPLEY SLAVICEK

## CHELSEA HOUSE
*An Infobase Learning Company*

## The Boer War

Chelsea House
An imprint of Infobase Learning
132 West 31st Street
New York, NY 10001

**Library of Congress Cataloging-in-Publication Data**

Slavicek, Louise Chipley, 1956-
The Boer War / by Louise Chipley Slavicek.
  p.  cm. — (Milestones in modern world history)
Includes bibliographical references and index.
ISBN-13: 978-1-60413-458-2 (hardcover)
ISBN-10: 1-60413-458-5 (hardcover)
1. South African War, 1899–1902—Juvenile literature. 2. Great Britain—Colonies—Africa—History—Juvenile literature. 3. South Africa—Politics and government—1836-1909—Juvenile literature. I. Title. II. Series: Milestones in modern world history.

DT1896.S625  2011
968.048—dc22                    2011004477

Chelsea House books are available at special discounts when purchased in bulk quantities for businesses, associations, institutions, or sales promotions. Please call our Special Sales Department in New York at (212) 967-8800 or (800) 322-8755.

You can find Chelsea House on the World Wide Web at http://www.infobaselearning.com.

Text design by Erik Lindstrom
Cover design by Alicia Post
Composition by Keith Trego
Cover printed by Bang Printing, Brainerd, Minn.
Book printed and bound by Bang Printing, Brainerd, Minn.
Date printed: September 2011
Printed in the United States of America

10 9 8 7 6 5 4 3 2 1

This book is printed on acid-free paper.

All links and Web addresses were checked and verified to be correct at the time of publication. Because of the dynamic nature of the Web, some addresses and links may have changed since publication and may no longer be valid.

# CONTENTS

# Boers, Britons, and Native Africans

When the Boer War between Great Britain and the white-controlled South African republics of the Transvaal and Orange Free State erupted on October 11, 1899, popular opinion on both sides of the conflict optimistically predicted that the fighting would be over by Christmas. Little could either the British or the Boers—the republics' chiefly Dutch-descended white inhabitants—have imagined then that the war would drag on for nearly three years and claim the lives of some 30,000 soldiers and an estimated 48,000 noncombatants, most of them children.

## BOER VERSUS BRITON

The Boer War was the culmination of decades of tension between the Boers, who had first settled the Cape Colony on

Africa's southern tip in 1652, and the British, who had annexed the Cape in 1814. By the mid-1830s, thousands of Boer farmers, deeply dissatisfied with British rule, trekked northward out of the Cape to the velds, or grasslands, of South Africa's interior, where they founded the independent sister republics of the Transvaal and Orange Free State. Until vast gold deposits were discovered in the Transvaal in 1886, the British showed relatively little interest in South Africa's drought-ridden interior, focusing their attention instead on the region's commercially and strategically important coastal areas. When the Transvaal suddenly emerged as the world's leading gold producer during the late 1880s, however, British leaders in both the Cape and in London began to see the Boer states in a very different light.

In the late 1800s, Great Britain was not only one of the world's foremost trading and military powers but also the ruler of the largest empire in human history, spanning seven continents and including colonies in many different parts of Africa. Maintaining the empire's standing among other imperialist powers, especially Germany, which had recently acquired several African colonies, was a major concern for Britain's government, then led by the Conservative Party. When the discovery of extensive goldfields in the Transvaal transformed the country into Africa's new economic powerhouse, British officials worried that the little republic could all too easily fall under the sway of Germany or one of the empire's other chief rivals. Determined to prevent that from occurring, they sought to bring the Transvaal firmly within the British orbit, by force if necessary. Using as their excuse a long-standing political dispute between the Boer government and the thousands of British prospectors who flocked to the Transvaal's gold mines from 1886 on, British leaders began sending large numbers of additional troops to South Africa during the summer of 1899.

Fearful that the British were planning to invade the Transvaal after London ignored their demands to withdraw all troops from their borders, Boer leaders in the Transvaal and

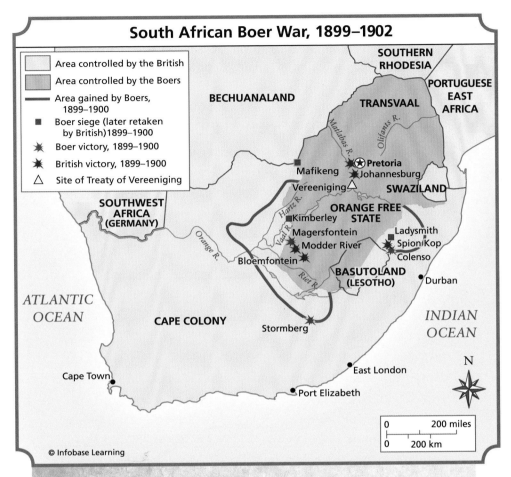

## South African Boer War, 1899–1902

Area controlled by the British

Area controlled by the Boers

Area gained by Boers, 1899–1900

■ Boer siege (later retaken by British)1899–1900

✳ Boer victory, 1899–1900

✳ British victory, 1899–1900

△ Site of Treaty of Vereeniging

SOUTHERN RHODESIA

PORTUGUESE EAST AFRICA

BECHUANALAND

TRANSVAAL

Matlabas R.

Olifants R.

■ Mafikeng

✳ ⊛ Pretoria
✳ Johannesburg

Vereeniging △

SWAZILAND

SOUTHWEST AFRICA (GERMANY)

Hartz R.

ORANGE FREE STATE

■ Kimberley

Vaal R.

Orange R.

✳ Magersfontein

✳ Modder River

Ladysmith

■ Spion Kop

Colenso

Bloemfontein ✳

Riat R.

BASUTOLAND (LESOTHO)

• Durban

ATLANTIC OCEAN

CAPE COLONY

✳ Stormberg

INDIAN OCEAN

N

• East London

Cape Town •

• Port Elizabeth

0        200 miles
0        200 km

© Infobase Learning

The Boer War (1899–1902)—also known as the Second Boer War or the Anglo-Boer South African War—was fought between the British Empire and the Afrikaans-speaking inhabitants of the independent Boer republics of the South African Republic (Transvaal Republic) and the Orange Free State. This map of southern Africa shows British- and Boer-controlled territories and identifies the major events of the Boer War.

its close ally, the Orange Free State, declared war on Britain in October 1899. Because the British army proved unable to defeat the much smaller Boer commando force for nearly three years, the Boer War, or the War for Independence, (as the Boers preferred to call the conflict), was not only Britain's bloodiest war but also its most humiliating since the Napoleonic Wars

(1803–1815). As a result of British commander in chief Lord Kitchener's ruthless policies toward Boer civilians, it was also destined to be one of the most controversial wars in all of English history.

## THE ANGLO-BOER SOUTH AFRICAN WAR

Although the Boer War's origins lay in a power struggle between two white groups—the Boers and the Britons—for control of the land and resources of central South Africa, it was not a "white man's war," as the conflict was once commonly described. In fact, as most scholars of the Boer War now agree, directly or indirectly, the conflict impacted the lives of virtually all the region's nearly one million black inhabitants.

Between October 1899 and the war's end on May 31, 1902, native South Africans were drawn into the fighting on both the British and the Boer sides. An estimated 100,000 blacks provided invaluable assistance to the British army as guards, messengers, spies, drivers, and scouts. At least 10,000 blacks served with Boer commando units as porters, cooks, or laborers. Hundreds of thousands of native Africans were left in desperate economic straits by the war. Many lost their sole means of support when the gold mines that had employed them before October 1899 were closed for the duration of the fighting. Others lost their homes as well as their livelihoods when British troops destroyed their farms, livestock, and villages as part of a systematic scorched-earth policy intended to force a Boer surrender by laying waste to large parts of the Transvaal and Free State. Some 120,000 of the homeless blacks ended up in primitive refugee or "concentration" camps run by the British army, where as many as 20,000 people, most of them children under the age of 16, are believed to have perished from disease or malnutrition.

The shockingly high death rate, primarily from contagious diseases such as typhoid and dysentery, among the thousands of homeless Boer families in the crowded white concentration camps was widely publicized at the time and has been detailed in countless histories of the Boer War ever since. Yet it was not until well into the twentieth century that most scholars even became aware of the considerably less well-documented black refugee camps' equally horrific conditions. In 1999, five years after South Africa's black majority finally won control of their country after 150 years of white rule, the government proclaimed a new nationally inclusive (if somewhat unwieldy) name for the Boer War in belated recognition of black involvement in the conflict: the Anglo-Boer South African War.

# The Boer War's Deep Roots

The roots of the Boer War stretch back more than three centuries to the beginnings of European colonization in the present-day Republic of South Africa. Africa's southern tip had been important to European navigators and traders since 1488, when the Portuguese explorer, Bartolomeu Dias, opened the sea route to India and the Far East by successfully rounding the Cape of Good Hope. Nonetheless, not until 1652 would the first European settlement be founded in southern Africa. That April, the Dutch East India Company, a private trading corporation with close ties to the Netherlands government, sent their employee Jan van Riebeeck to the Cape of Good Hope, accompanied by 90 colonists. Van Riebeeck's assignment was to establish a fortified way station for the company's profitable trade route to Asia, particularly Indonesia's Spice Islands, on

12

This painting depicts Jan van Riebeeck's landing at the Cape of Good Hope in 1652. Van Riebeeck led a Dutch expedition to the southernmost part of Africa and established a colony there.

the site of what would eventually become the bustling port city of Cape Town.

## THE BOERS

As far as the officials of the Dutch East India Company were concerned, the Cape Colony's overriding purpose was to provide a source of fresh vegetables and fruit to the crews of the organization's trading vessels on their long voyages from Holland to the exotic markets of the East. Within a decade of their arrival in Cape Town, however, some of the Dutch colonists had abandoned the settlement's company-run gardens and orchards to labor on their own farm fields and pasturelands well beyond the town's boundaries and the trading corporation's control. During the late 1600s, these independent-minded Dutch farmers were joined by 200 Huguenot (French Protestant) immigrants, who were fleeing religious persecution in their Catholic homeland.

Like the new Huguenot settlers, the Dutch settlers of the Cape's hinterlands were devoted followers of John Calvin, the sixteenth-century French Protestant reformer. Calvin's religious teachings stressed the absolute righteousness of God and the complete sinfulness of humanity. Calvin is today best known for his doctrine of predestination, in which he asserted that divine forgiveness and salvation were not open to all people or even all Christians, not even those who conducted their lives

## A "CHOSEN PEOPLE"

A central element of the Boers' evolving cultural identity was their belief that like the ancient Israelites of the Bible, they were a "chosen people" selected by God to create a holy society in their African promised land. They believed the velds (open grasslands of South Africa) where they constructed their farmhouses, grazed their cattle, and planted their crops, had been specially set aside for them by God. The fact that most of the Cape was already being used as pastureland or hunting grounds by the area's indigenous peoples, the Khoikhoi and the San, did not trouble them. The Boers, or Afrikaners, as they were also starting to be called during the eighteenth century, were certain that the African lands they tilled and grazed were for them alone.

according to the moral rules set down in Scripture. Instead, Calvin argued, God had "predestined," or foreordained, certain souls for redemption and eternal life and others for eternal damnation from before the dawn of time.

Drawn together by their Calvinist principles, including a staunch faith in the virtues of hard work, economic self-reliance, and frugality, the Dutch and Huguenot pioneers of the Cape's hinterlands soon intermarried. By the mid-1700s, they were well on their way to developing a distinctive Boer ("farmer" in Dutch) cultural identity, firmly grounded in their uncompromising religious and moral beliefs. The Boers even had their own dialect, Afrikaans, a name taken from the Dutch word for African. Based chiefly on Dutch, Afrikaans was also influenced by French, several indigenous African languages, and German,

Adding to the Boers' sense of entitlement regarding their adopted homeland was a deep-seated conviction that the region's original inhabitants were inherently and irrevocably inferior to them. According to their biased interpretation of religious scripture, whites were spiritually, morally, and intellectually superior to nonwhites. Consequently, it was only natural that whites should rule over all the other races of mankind. Because of the Afrikaners' racist ideology, when the veld's indigenous peoples resisted the Boers' authority, either by stubbornly remaining on land claimed by the white settlers or by refusing to toil as virtual slaves on white farms, the Calvinist pioneers felt justified in killing them. Tragically, a little more than a century after the Boers began leaving Cape Town for the surrounding countryside, violent encounters with musket-toting settlers, in combination with smallpox and other imported European diseases, had all but wiped out the area's Khoikhoi and San populations.

owing to an influx of German-speaking Protestant settlers to the Cape during the eighteenth century.

## THE COMING OF THE BRITISH

Nearly a century and a half after the founding of Cape Town, the British—South Africa's second-major European colonizing group—arrived in great numbers in the Dutch port. The French Revolutionary Wars (1792–1802) were raging in Europe, and French troops had recently occupied the Netherlands. In 1795, determined to protect their country's growing interests in India and the Far East, British leaders dispatched a fleet of warships and several thousand men to the Cape to ensure that this critical port on the eastern sea route remained safely out of French hands. After the Peace of Amiens between France and Great Britain brought their war to a close in early 1802, British troops voluntarily withdrew from the Cape, and Holland resumed control of the colony. The Anglo-French peace was to prove short-lived, however. In 1806, with the Netherlands firmly under the sway of France's emperor, Napoleon Bonaparte, London decided to send a large new occupying force to Cape Town.

In 1815, after Napoleon's army was decisively defeated at the Battle of Waterloo, Europe was once again at peace. This time, however, London did not offer to return the Cape Colony to Holland. Instead, after paying the Dutch government £6 million in compensation, Britain formally annexed all of the Netherlands' territories in southern Africa. British officials had concluded that the Cape had simply become too valuable to lose because of its strategic location as the only feasible route to England's expanding empire in India and to the lucrative markets of East Asia.

## A CLASH OF CULTURES

From the outset, relations between the Afrikaners and their new British overlords were strained. The English officials' policy of "introducing a British way of life and British values to the Colony quickly roused the hostility of the Boers," observes historian David Smurthwaite. "English rather than Dutch became the official language," he writes, "immigration from Britain was encouraged, and a number of what were seen by the Boers as anti-Dutch laws were introduced."[1]

Largely left alone by the Dutch East India Company and Netherlands government to do as they pleased, the Boers bitterly resented Britain's more hands-on approach to colonial administration, particularly in the realm of race relations. During the 1820s, British officials approved a series of laws designed to ensure the more humane treatment of the Colony's heavily exploited black and "colored" (mixed race) servants, much to the Boers' dismay. According to the new legislation, which had been urged on by the English missionaries to the Cape, all alleged lawbreakers—regardless of their race—had to be brought before a court of law. Boer farmers could no longer administer floggings or other forms of corporal punishment to wayward nonwhite servants. Additionally, for the first time, free black and colored inhabitants of the Cape were allowed to own land, could no longer be forced to enter into labor contracts, and did not have to carry special passes from their employers whenever they left his or her property.

In 1833, after the British Parliament officially abolished slavery throughout the empire, Boer dissatisfaction with their English rulers reached new heights. Chattel slavery had existed in the Cape Colony almost from its founding. Worried about the fledgling settlement's ability to survive in a hostile environment, the Dutch East India Company at first forbade colonists from enslaving their Khoikhoi and San neighbors, importing nonwhite slaves into the Cape from other parts of Africa and the Netherlands' colonies in Southeast Asia instead. Many of these slaves or their descendants eventually ended up toiling on Boer farms. By the time the British annexed the Cape, slave ownership had become widespread among Afrikaners, although few colonists could afford to own more than a few bondmen or -women.

Historian Gregory Fremont-Barnes asserts that from the Boers' viewpoint, London's insistence on banning slavery in the Cape amounted to an unconscionable "interference in their way of life," one that "not only threatened them economically, but introduced an element of democracy inconsistent with the Boers' sense of their own racial superiority."[2] Britain's "shameful and unjust" emancipation policies, accused Anna Steenkamp, a member of a prominent Boer family, threatened to place the colony's "heathen" (in other words, nonwhite) population "on an equal footing with Christians, contrary to the laws of God, and the natural distinction of race and religion."[3] Britain's plan for reimbursing slave owners for their lost "property" only added to the Boers' outrage. Not only was the amount of the compensation woefully inadequate, the Afrikaners complained, but the monies could only be collected in London, 6,000 miles away.

## THE GREAT TREK

Hoping to escape British control while at the same time acquiring new lands for their expanding population, disgruntled Boer settlers began leaving the Cape Colony in the mid-1830s, in what came to be known in Afrikaner folklore as the Great Trek. Between about 1834 and 1843, as many as 15,000 Boers, representing nearly half the Cape's non-British white population, headed out of the colony. "They took everything they needed with them," writes historian Thomas Pakenham, "their sheep and their cattle, enough guns and gunpowder to subdue the natives, and enough resentment against the British to last a century."[4] Trekking north- and northeastward in great ox-drawn canvas-covered wagons, many of the emigrants pushed into the fertile coastal region of Natal, while others journeyed inland toward the Orange and Vaal rivers. Along the way the *voortrekkers* (Afrikaans for "pioneers") confronted numerous hardships

In the 1830s and 1840s, in what came to be known as the Great Trek, Boer farmers sought to escape British rule by moving away from the Cape Colony and northward to the Transvaal.

and dangers, including frequent attacks by the areas' indigenous peoples, most notably the powerful Zulus.

The voortrekkers' success in planting new settlements in the South African wilderness in the late 1830s and early 1840s, despite enormous obstacles and perils, was a defining moment in the history of the Afrikaners. After the Great Trek, they established three independent Boer communities in Natal, the Transvaal (meaning "across the Vaal"), and between the Orange and Vaal rivers. More than ever, the Boers felt assured of God's special favor to them. Smurthwaite writes:

> For the settlers, with their Biblical attitude to life, the Great
> Trek was a unifying influence of considerable significance.
> It brought home to them the belief that they were a chosen
> people who had an opportunity to create an embracing
> Boer identity based upon an independent state governed by
> God's will.[5]

The courageous resolve of the voortrekkers, as they battled epidemic disease, exhaustion, and hostile natives to preserve their way of life from what they viewed as the corrupting sway of the British, quickly became the stuff of legend within the Boer community. By encouraging a profound sense of national consciousness, pride, and destiny among the Afrikaners, the Great Trek would play a crucial role in shaping future Anglo-Boer interactions.

## BRITAIN AND THE VOORTREKKERS

Although British colony officials made no effort to stop the voortrekkers from departing the Cape, they insisted that the Boer emigrants were still British subjects and thus under their jurisdiction. In 1843, determined to maintain tight control over the strategically and commercially valuable South African coastline, the British government formally annexed Natal, spurring a new exodus of disgruntled Boer farmers inland to the fledgling voortrekker settlements beyond the Orange and Vaal rivers.

Consisting chiefly of scrubby grasslands and continually threatened by hostile indigenous peoples, the new Boer settlements in the South African interior held little appeal for the British. "For imperial interest," remarks historian Bill Nasson, "nothing very much hung on them."[6] By the early 1850s, having concluded that any attempt to control the voortrekkers' inland territories would be a waste of the empire's financial and military resources, London formally recognized the independence of the pioneer Boer communities to the north of the Orange and the Vaal rivers. Across the Vaal in the northernmost part of the modern-day Republic of South Africa, the British officially granted self-rule to the Afrikaner farmers of the Transvaal by the Sand (Zand) River Convention of 1852. Two years later, the Bloemfontein Convention did the same for the scattered Boer settlements between the Vaal and the Orange rivers, now united as the Orange Free State.

As much as they may have wished to, however, the Boers of the Transvaal and Orange Free State could not entirely sever their ties with Great Britain. According to the Conventions of 1852 and 1854, Britain retained ultimate control over the two states' foreign affairs. Furthermore, the British insisted that involuntary servitude be outlawed in the Afrikaner republics. Despite their firm stand against slavery, British officials made no effort to interfere with the Afrikaner governments' other racist policies. As might be expected given the Boers' profoundly racist ideology, nonwhites in the two republics were excluded from voting and denied even the most basic civil rights. In contrast, in the British colonies of Natal and the Cape, black and mixed-race residents were awarded full citizenship and, at least in theory, complete equality before the law. Yet, while better off legally and economically than their downtrodden counterparts in the Transvaal and Orange Free State, nonwhite inhabitants of the Cape and Natal still faced widespread racial discrimination, particularly within the job market. Most could not earn enough to meet the colonies' financial qualifications for voting.

## A LUCRATIVE DISCOVERY

In the late 1860s, the chance discovery of vast diamond deposits near Kimberley along the Cape Colony's northern fringes drew thousands of fortune seekers to the borderlands between the Orange Free State and the Cape. It also rekindled Britain's interest in the arid and conflict-ridden South African interior, which only a decade earlier London had happily handed over to the voortrekkers.

Since the diamond fields were located on land claimed by both the Orange Free State and the Cape Colony, the lucrative mineral discovery created a significant new source of friction between Boer and British leaders. In 1871, despite angry protests from President Johannes Brand of the Orange Free State and other Boer leaders, Great Britain annexed the disputed diamond zone around Kimberley, also known as Griqualand West, in honor of the Griqua, a local African people. At Brand's urging, London eventually agreed in 1876 to pay the Orange Free State £90,000 pounds for the loss of Griqualand West. By this time, however, "the Boers harbored great suspicions of British intentions in South Africa," notes Fremont-Barnes.[7] The Boers' suspicions were confirmed just one year later when, in violation of the Sand River Convention, the British government annexed the Transvaal Republic.

## A CONFEDERATION SCHEME

Britain's annexation of the Transvaal in 1877 was a direct consequence of its leaders' growing interest in the South African interior since diamonds had been discovered in the borderlands between the Orange Free State and the Cape Colony. From the very beginning of the empire's involvement in South Africa, British leaders had focused almost exclusively on maintaining control over its coastal regions in order to keep open the vital sea route between Europe and Asia. In the eyes of many British officials, Griqualand West's vast mineral deposits, along with reports of possible goldfields in the Transvaal, had greatly increased the economic and strategic importance of all of South Africa for the British Empire.

By the mid-1870s, two of Britain's most imperialistic officials, the colonial secretary, Lord Carnarvon, and the high commissioner for Southern Africa, Henry Bartle Frere, were determined to bring the Transvaal and Orange Free State, along with the rest of southern Africa, firmly into the British orbit. They believed uniting South Africa's various colonies, republics, and tribal chiefdoms under British rule was the best way for the empire to exploit the region's valuable natural resources while also safeguarding it against potential threats from the increasingly expansionist German Reich and other imperialistic foreign powers. To accomplish this ambitious goal, Carnarvon and Frere proposed creating a confederation within the British Empire of the Cape, Natal, Griqualand West, and all South African territories currently controlled by the Boers or indigenous African groups.

The logical first step in their confederation scheme, Carnarvon and Frere quickly concluded, was to annex the larger and more populous of the two Boer republics in the South African interior, the Transvaal. By the 1870s, inefficient administration combined with a series of expensive armed conflicts with local black peoples had left the government of the Transvaal on the brink of bankruptcy. The turmoil also destroyed popular confidence in the leadership of its president, Thomas Burgers. Carnarvon and Frere reasoned that if the British pledged to devote their formidable military and financial resources to crushing the Transvaalers' African enemies, particularly the Zulus to their east, Burgers and his colleagues in the beleaguered government in Pretoria might be persuaded to go along with annexation. Once the Transvaal joined the British Empire, they optimistically predicted, it seemed likely its smaller Boer neighbor to the south, the Orange Free State, would follow suit.

## THE NEW BRITISH COLONY OF THE TRANSVAAL

In late January 1877, British diplomat Sir Theophilus Shepstone and a small force of 25 men arrived in the Transvaal capital of Pretoria to urge President Burgers to accept annexation as the only viable solution to the state's pressing security and financial problems. Just as Carnarvon and Frere had hoped, with the Transvaal treasury nearly empty and the armies of the Zulu kingdom menacing the republic from the east, Shepstone's proposal encountered only token resistance in Pretoria. Without a single shot being fired, and less than three months after the British emissary's arrival in the capital, "the Union Jack was flying over the government buildings of the new British colony of the Transvaal," writes Pakenham.[8] Shepstone's formal proclamation of Britain's annexation of the Transvaal on April 12, 1877, was greeted with mostly stoic resignation by its citizens. For the time being, Afrikaners were prepared to submit to the humiliating new political arrangement with their chief European rival as a matter of sheer survival.

In January 1879, the Transvaal's new rulers let loose the armies of the British Empire on the Boers' native African enemies. That month the British declared war on the Zulu, the colony's most formidable adversary. Despite the Zulus' unexpected early triumph at the Battle of Isandlwana, on July 4, 1879, British forces decisively defeated their *impi* ("warriors") at the Battle of Ulundi, bringing the war—and the Zulu military threat in South Africa—to an abrupt end.

With the military might of their foremost African foe broken, Transvaalers underwent a major change of heart regarding their earlier willingness to sacrifice their independence in return for the protection of the British army. After all, it had been their deep disdain for the alien culture and values of their British rulers that had driven the Transvaal Boers into the perilous wilderness of the South African interior. In the wake of the overwhelming Zulu loss at Ulundi, the Afrikaners' self-appointed British defenders now looked like more than occupiers, and "the Boers' powerful tradition of nationalism, temporarily paralyzed by an empty treasury and the Zulu menace, was suddenly given new life," contends Pakenham.[9]

During the months following the end of the Anglo-Zulu War, popular resentment against British rule crystallized around the former Transvaal Republic's ardently nationalistic and deeply religious vice president, Paul Kruger. An outspoken critic of annexation beginning in mid-1877, Kruger had made the long journey to London to protest what he viewed as Britain's unlawful takeover of the Transvaal. In April 1880, after William Gladstone, an outspoken critic of recent British policies in South Africa, became prime minister of Great Britain, Kruger gained new hope that the hated annexation would be revoked. Kruger, however, was to be bitterly disappointed. Despite his own anti-imperialist leanings, Gladstone realized that his ministers were sharply divided over whether to award the Transvaal more freedom. Eager to keep his cabinet's unity, he decided to maintain the status quo in the former Boer republic, at least for the time being.

Gladstone's refusal to grant the Transvaal even limited self-rule proved to be the last straw for Kruger and for the growing Boer resistance movement. By late 1880, convinced that additional negotiations with the British government were pointless, Kruger and other prominent nationalist political figures—including the former Transvaal Republic's first president, Marthinus Pretorius, and attorney general, Piet Joubert—resolved to rise in armed rebellion against their homeland's powerful overlords. "The general conviction was now arrived at that further meetings and friendly protests were useless," Kruger later explained in his memoirs. "The best course appeared to be to set quietly to work and to prepare for the worst by the purchase of arms and ammunition."[10]

# A Successful Revolt and a Failed Raid

On December 13, 1880, Paul Kruger, Piet Joubert, and Marthinus Pretorius boldly proclaimed the Transvaal's independence from Great Britain. Three days later, Boer forces attacked the British army garrison at Potchefstroom in the southern Transvaal, launching what would become known as the Transvaal War or First Boer War.

## THE TRANSVAAL WAR

By the beginning of January 1881, the rebellious Boers had laid siege to all of the British garrisons scattered throughout the Transvaal. Nonetheless, high-ranking English army officials, including Major-General George Pomeroy Colley, commander of British forces in southeastern Africa, failed to take the Afrikaners' military capabilities seriously. After all, they reasoned, the Transvaalers did not even possess a regular army. What the

The Transvaal War—also known as the First Boer War—was fought between the British and the Boers from December 1880 to March 1881. Here, Boer marksmen are depicted in battle against the British during that war.

Transvaalers did have, however, was a highly effective civilian militia system, as Pomeroy Colley and his colleagues in the imperial army would soon discover.

At the core of the Boers' carefully organized civilian militia system was the commando. Every administrative district within the Transvaal had its own commando unit, in which all white male residents between the ages of 16 and 60 were legally obliged to serve. Although the Afrikaner commandos had no formal uniforms and were expected to furnish their own horses, supplies, and rifles, they nevertheless constituted a formidable fighting force. The civilian warriors of the Transvaal outnumbered the 1,800 regular British troops stationed in the colony by nearly four to one, and most were also superb marksmen. Marksmanship, along with stealth and mobility—in which the commandos excelled as well—had been vital to the survival of the Transvaal's overwhelmingly rural population over the years, both for hunting game on the veld and for protecting the Boers' far-flung settlements against hostile native groups.

To the dismay of the British, all the short-lived Transvaal War's main engagements ended in defeat for the imperial army, a consequence of their opponents' marksmanship skills and more sophisticated understanding of the local terrain, as well as of their own flawed leadership and communications. During the imperial army's final humiliating rout at Majuba Hill near the Transvaal-Natal border on February 27, 1881, nearly 300 British troops were killed or wounded, while the 150-man Transvaal volunteer force suffered just 6 casualties. Among the British casualties was General Pomeroy Colley, who was killed by Boer sharpshooters as he attempted to rally his frantically retreating troops. Six days after the imperial army's devastating defeat at Majuba Hill, and not quite three months after the first shots of the Transvaal War were fired, General Henry Evelyn Wood, the new British commander for southeastern Africa, signed an armistice as the first step to peace negotiations. Historian Michael Barthorp notes:

> In terms of duration and numbers engaged on both sides—less than a thousand in all—Majuba Hill was little more than a skirmish. . . . Yet its effects were far-reaching.

For the victors each individual Boer's yearning for unfettered personal independence became transformed into an aggressive and unified Afrikaner nationalism all over South Africa. On the vanquished it inflicted a festering wound of bitterness and humiliation which could be healed only by revenge.[1]

## PEACE AND A REBORN TRANSVAAL REPUBLIC

In April 1880, William Gladstone refused to even consider Paul Kruger's request to revoke the Transvaal's annexation. The prime minister had been repeatedly assured by British military officials that the Transvaalers would not try to take on the largest empire in the world in order to secure their independence and would be quickly subdued if they did. Consequently, although Gladstone had little enthusiasm for Britain's recent imperialistic ventures in the Transvaal or in Africa generally, he sought to put off dealing with the divisive issue of what to do about the colony and its disgruntled Boer inhabitants for as long as possible.

In February 1881, in the wake of the British army's third major battlefield loss against the Transvaalers at Majuba, Gladstone at last "decided enough was enough," maintains Barthorp.[2] Convinced that Britain had already squandered too much of its financial and military resources attempting to hang onto a distant, poor, and agrarian colony, Gladstone repealed the annexation and approved a compromise peace settlement with the Boers. He did this despite the objections of his more imperialistic colleagues in the British government.

According to the Pretoria Convention of August 3, 1881, the Transvaal was no longer a crown colony, although London still had the last say regarding the state's foreign affairs. Under the Convention's terms, Britain was also to oversee all of the restored republic's domestic legislation pertaining to its black population. London reserved this right after hearing reports that Boer farmers had been abducting black children from the veld and forcing them into long "apprenticeships" that amounted to little more than slavery. In the Convention's preamble (or opening statement), the Gladstone government, apparently in an effort to placate the imperialists, also insisted on including a reference to the "suzerainty [or dominion] of Her Majesty [Queen Victoria]" over the Transvaal.[3] Just what this dominion over the Boer state actually entailed, however, was never explained in the peace agreement.

Although Kruger, Joubert, and Pretorius, the triumvirate who had proclaimed the Transvaal's independence in December 1880, agreed to assume formal leadership of the reborn republic one week after the signing of the Pretoria Convention, they had serious reservations regarding the settlement's requirements. The proud and intensely pro-Afrikaner Kruger, who was elected as president of the Transvaal in 1883, was determined to renegotiate the peace settlement. More than anything else, he wanted to bring an end to what he considered as Britain's arrogant meddling in his homeland's affairs.

Soon after his inauguration, Kruger set sail for London to urge the Gladstone government to approve a new Anglo-Boer peace agreement, one that he hoped would finally free the Transvaal from British influence. Preoccupied with what he considered as far more pressing problems closer to home in Ireland, where a powerful nationalist movement was developing, Gladstone agreed to throw out the Pretoria Convention and start afresh. In the new London Convention of February 1884, Gladstone made several important concessions to Kruger. He granted the Boer regime complete control over domestic matters and expunged from the settlement any mention of the queen's "suzerainty" over the Boer state. Nonetheless, despite Kruger's objections, Gladstone, citing his nation's status as the preeminent power in southern Africa, reserved Britain's right to review any future treaties drawn up by the Transvaalers with any country other than the Orange Free State or with neighboring African tribes.

The international face of Boer resistance against the British Empire was Paul Kruger, who played a leading part in fighting the permanent annexation of the South African Republic (Transvaal). Kruger served as president of the republic from May 1883 to September 1900.

## A GOLD RUSH IN THE TRANSVAAL

When the British signed the London Convention, no one in London foresaw the extraordinary discovery that would be made in the Transvaal almost exactly two years later. In March 1886, just to the south of Pretoria in a barren expanse of high veld known as the Witwatersrand (Rand for short), an English prospector by the name of George Harrison stumbled across the rocky outcrop of a gold reef of spectacular proportions. (The high veld is the high-altitude grassland region of eastern South Africa.) Within a few years, the Rand had become the most productive gold mining region in the world. Soon foreign prospectors, miners, and businessmen, most of them British subjects, were flooding into the Transvaal by the tens of thousands. Almost overnight, the bustling mining town of Johannesburg sprouted up in the Witwatersrand's once desolate hills. By 1890, Johannesburg was the largest city in all of southern Africa with a population of more than 25,000, the majority of whom were British nationals.

Although the revenue generated by the Rand's treasure trove proved an enormous boon for the cash-strapped Transvaal government, Kruger and many of his fellow Afrikaners viewed Harrison's lucrative discovery as a decidedly mixed blessing. They feared that the massive waves of gold-hungry *uitlanders* (Afrikaans for "outsiders" or "foreigners") descending on the Transvaal posed a grave threat to the Boers' distinctive and, in their judgment, ethically and spiritually superior way of life. Fremont-Barnes writes:

> Possessing alien ideas on morality, religion, business practices and education, these economic immigrants brought in their wake a host of vices attendant on a rapidly growing economy: gambling, prostitution and violence. Worse still, the Uitlanders were thought to threaten not only the traditional moral and religious base of Afrikaner society, but the very political system of the Transvaal. The Uitlanders,

One of the major sources of conflict leading up to the Boer War was the discovery of gold in South Africa. Seen here, an 1887 graphic taken from the *Illustrated London News* of a water-powered stamping mill for crushing gold ore.

if granted political rights, could by their very numbers have swamped the Afrikaner population and refashioned society completely through the extension of the vote. This could, for instance, have led to some form of limited franchise for blacks, which already existed in the Cape Colony, an idea that was unthinkable to the Boers.[4]

In 1890, to prevent this scenario from becoming reality, the Volksraad, the Transvaal's legislative assembly, dramatically upped the residency requirement for voting in presidential and Volksraad elections from five to 14 years. Kruger made sure that the uitlanders were hemmed in by economic as well as political restrictions by refusing to grant the immigrants concessions for vital mining equipment or railway transport. To add insult to injury, the uitlanders, despite being denied political representation, were burdened with a wide range of duties and taxes, including a particularly heavy tax on the dynamite essential for blasting open the Rand's mines.

## CECIL RHODES AND THE UITLANDERS

In the early 1890s, Britain-born financier and South African diamond magnate Cecil Rhodes observed the growing animosity between the chiefly British uitlanders and the Transvaal's Boer rulers with keen interest. Rhodes was not only one of the richest men in the world but had been, since 1890, the Cape Colony's chief executive or premier. "Cecil Rhodes, like Paul Kruger, was a man with a mission," historian Brian Roberts asserts.[5] Whereas Kruger believed that God had specially chosen the Boers to build their society in the African wilderness, the imperialistic Rhodes thought the British were "the first race in the world, and that the more of the world we inhabit the better it is for the human race." In 1877, as a fledgling entrepreneur and college student dividing his time between Kimberley's diamond fields and England's Oxford University, Rhodes had pledged himself to labor for the "furtherance of the British Empire, for the bringing of the whole uncivilized world under British rule." Rhodes was especially anxious for the British to incorporate the vast and mineral-rich continent of Africa into their extensive empire: "Africa is still lying ready for us [and] it is our duty to take it."[6]

In 1885, in keeping with his self-proclaimed goal of "painting as much of Africa British red as possible," Rhodes played a key role in securing imperial rule over the territories west of the Transvaal known as Bechuanaland (now Botswana).[7] Then, in 1889, after Rhodes tricked local tribal leaders into granting him exclusive mineral rights in what are today the nations of Zimbabwe and Zambia, Queen Victoria granted his British South Africa Company a protectorate over the territories north of the Transvaal, which he soon set about

# CECIL RHODES

One of nine children of an Anglican clergyman, Cecil John Rhodes was born in Bishop's Stortford, England, on July 5, 1853. A sickly child, he was packed off as a teenager to live with his older brother, a Natal cotton farmer, in hopes that his fragile health would improve in South Africa's warmer climate. Not long after Rhodes's arrival in Africa, Kimberley's vast diamond deposits were discovered. In 1871, 18-year-old Rhodes, eager to make his fortune, abandoned farming to become a prospector in the diamond fields. By the end of the following decade, his remarkable success as a prospector and later as a diamond-claim speculator had made him one of the wealthiest men in the world.

Rhodes's political career began in 1880 when he was elected to the Cape Parliament. Within eight years, the ambitious mining magnate had risen to the post of colony premier. After his involvement in the Jameson Raid led to his forced resignation from the premiership in January 1896, Rhodes focused most of his energy on developing Rhodesia. When he died at age 48 on March 26, 1902, it was discovered that Rhodes had left most of his fortune to Oxford University to create a scholarship for students from the British colonies, the United States, and Germany to study at the renowned English university. Today, more than 90 Rhodes Scholars are chosen worldwide each year; more than 7,000 scholarships have been awarded since the fellowship was first instituted.

colonizing with British nationals. Six years later, impatient to bring even more of Africa under British sway, Rhodes focused his attention on the Transvaal itself, where he thought he detected in the discontent of the uitlanders an opportunity for the British Empire to regain control of its mineral-rich former colony.

Sometime in late 1895, Rhodes secretly approached the leaders of an immigrant organization in Johannesburg dedicated to obtaining greater political rights for uitlanders through constitutional reform. After years of petition writing and protest meetings, the group had not convinced the Kruger regime to amend its stringent voting requirements. Consequently, when Rhodes promised to provide rifles and armed support to the organization if it rose in rebellion against the Boer government, many of the frustrated reformers were ready to give his daring proposal serious consideration. Rhodes was confident that once a full-scale uitlander revolt was underway in Johannesburg, the British government would send in troops to protect its subjects against the Boer commandos. Reasoning that Kruger would not risk a second war with Britain—particularly since the more imperialistic Lord Salisbury had recently replaced Gladstone as prime minister—Rhodes predicted that once British troops arrived in Johannesburg, Kruger would cave in to the rebels' demands for political representation. After the uitlanders were granted the franchise, Rhodes optimistically believed, it would just be a matter of time before the president and his Afrikaner cohorts were voted out of office and an administration receptive to reunification with the British Empire was voted in.

## THE JAMESON RAID

In December 1895, Rhodes launched his scheme to reestablish British control in the Transvaal by sending a force of nearly 500 heavily armed policemen from his company's protectorate in modern-day Zimbabwe and Zambia (which had recently been named Rhodesia in the mining magnate's honor) to Bechuanaland. Rhodes entrusted a longtime friend and business associate, Dr. Leander Starr Jameson, with leading the mounted force, which was to cross into the Boer republic from Bechuanaland as soon as the uitlanders rose up.

Back in Johannesburg, however, Jameson's immigrant collaborators were starting to get cold feet. By the end of the month, the immigrants had still not committed themselves to a particular date to begin the uprising. In truth, many of the uitlanders were uncertain about whether to go along with Rhodes's violent and potentially extremely risky plan at all. Finally, on December 29, an exasperated Jameson decided to take matters into his own hands. Without waiting for a final go-ahead from Rhodes, Jameson boldly led his police force over the Transvaal border and headed toward Johannesburg.

Jameson and his raiders never made it to the mining town. On the morning of January 2, 1896, a large Boer commando force confronted the conspirators at the Doornkop farm, less than 20 miles (32 kilometers) outside Johannesburg. After a brief skirmish in which 16 raiders and just one commando were killed, the uitlanders' would-be champions were summarily arrested and hauled off to prison in Pretoria. In the meantime, the hoped-for immigrant uprising in Johannesburg never materialized.

After Kruger agreed to hand over the raiders to British custody (despite objections from some members of his government), Jameson and his top officers were sent to London for trial and imprisoned. For his role in the plot, Rhodes was censured by Parliament and forced to resign as the Cape's premier. Despite London's public show of disapproval for the conspirators, however, Kruger and his fellow Boers were more distrustful than ever regarding Britain's true intentions in the Transvaal, and to southern Africa generally. Determined to protect his people's hard-won independence, Kruger beefed up the Transvaal's police force, constructed new garrisons, and increased state expenditures on armaments and ammunition fivefold in the wake of the Jameson Raid. Much of the money went to purchasing tens of thousands of state-of-the-art Mauser rifles from Germany for his state's commandos, who had previously been expected to furnish their own guns.

In 1897, Kruger also signed a mutual defense treaty with President Martinus Steyn of the Orange Free State. The unprec-

## KRUGER, THE KAISER, AND A POTENTIAL DIPLOMATIC CRISIS

As tensions between the Transvaal and Great Britain increased during the mid-1890s, Paul Kruger resolved to cultivate closer diplomatic links with Germany, Britain's chief economic and military rival in Europe. "If one nation [Britain] tries to kick us, the other [Germany] will try to stop it," the Transvaal president privately explained. Kruger promoted greater German investment in the Transvaal's booming gold industry and encouraged increased German immigration to the republic. In 1895, at a banquet in honor of Kaiser Wilhelm II, Kruger spoke in glowing terms of the deepening ties between his country and the German Empire, rattling political leaders in London as well as the fervently imperialist Cecil Rhodes in Cape Town.

Less than one year later, when news reached Berlin that the Transvaal government had repulsed Dr. Jameson's raid, the kaiser decided to show his support for the Boer Republic by sending Kruger a congratulatory telegram. The dispatch, published on January 3, read:

edented military alliance between the two fiercely independent republics testified to the growing sense of unity among South Africa's far-flung Afrikaner population following Jameson's failed invasion. In the late 1890s, this was a formidable population, which included approximately 250,000 Cape residents, 150,000 Transvaalers, 70,000 Orange Free Staters, and 10,000 Natalers. "Far from curbing Afrikaner power," as its perpetrators

---

I express to you my sincere congratulations that without calling on the aid of friendly Powers you and your people, by your own energy against the armed bands which have broken into your country as disturbers of the peace, have succeeded in reestablishing peace, and defending the independence of the country against attacks from without.

The kaiser's telegram created an uproar in the British press, since the message seemed to imply that if Kruger had asked his good friend, Germany, for military assistance against Jameson and his British raiders, the kaiser would have gladly obliged. Eager for a chance to flex some military muscle for the sake of the kaiser and Paul Kruger, Chamberlain persuaded Lord Salisbury to hold extensive naval maneuvers off the coast of South Africa. Meanwhile, back in London, Wilhelm's grandmother, Queen Victoria, felt compelled to scold the kaiser for his decidedly undiplomatic message. "I cannot refrain from expressing my deep regret at the telegram you sent President Kruger," she wrote. "It is considered very unfriendly towards this country, which I feel it is not intended to be, and has, I grieve to say, made a most unfortunate impression."*

* All quotations are from Meredith, **Diamonds, Gold, and War**, pp. 309, 345.

had hoped, Barthorp writes, "the Jameson Raid had strengthened and unified it."[8]

## CHAMBERLAIN AND MILNER'S IMPERIALISTIC DREAMS

British officials at home and in South Africa repeatedly
insisted that they had no foreknowledge of the Jameson Raid
in January 1896. Nevertheless, most historians now believe
that the recently appointed British colonial secretary, Joseph
Chamberlain, was aware of Rhodes's scheme, without tak-
ing an active role in its planning or execution. A committed
imperialist, Chamberlain, like Rhodes, hoped to bring as
much of Africa as possible under British rule, especially its
mineral-rich and strategically vital southern portion. To that
end, Chamberlain appointed Sir Alfred Milner as the new high
commissioner for Southern Africa in April 1897. Milner, an
outspoken imperialist, liked to refer to himself as "a civilian
soldier of the [British] Empire."[9]

Although careful to maintain a peacemaking stance toward
the Kruger government during his first months in office, Milner
was committed to regaining British control over the Transvaal.
Milner's determination to draw the Transvaal back within the
British sphere was lent a sense of urgency by his deep concerns
regarding the friendship that appeared to be developing, since
the Jameson Raid, between the Kruger regime and the world's
fastest-rising military power, the German Reich. Immediately
after the failed raid, Kaiser Wilhelm II of Germany sent a
widely publicized telegram to Kruger in which he warmly con-
gratulated the Boer leader on repelling the invasion. As Milner
well knew, the Germans had possessed a strong potential military base in southern Africa since 1884, when they annexed a
vast tract of land to the north of the Cape Colony and the west
of Bechuanaland (today the nation of Namibia). Consequently,
if Berlin and Pretoria's budding friendship led to a military
alliance between the two countries, Milner worried that his

dream of returning the Transvaal to the British fold might never be realized.

## "IT IS OUR COUNTRY YOU WANT!"

Milner was resolved to move as rapidly as possible with his plan to win back the Boer republic. In 1898, Milner began a campaign "to provoke the Transvaal into a crisis with Britain over the question of uitlanders' rights," contends Fremont-Barnes.[10] By demanding reform of the nation's franchise in the name of protecting the civil rights of the tens of thousands of British subjects residing in Johannesburg, Milner hoped he could goad Kruger into declaring war on the British Empire for a second time. With the more imperialistic Lord Salisbury as prime minister, Milner felt confident that the British government would be willing to crush the troublesome Boers once and for all and reclaim the empire's former colony.

Throughout 1898 and early 1899, Milner, with Chamberlain's backing, pressed Kruger to dramatically reduce the republic's residency requirements for citizenship. At the same time, he made sure that the uitlanders' grievances with the Kruger regime received a lot of publicity back in England, in an obvious effort to prepare the British public for the possibility of a second Transvaal war. In late May 1899, with neither Kruger nor Milner apparently willing to concede the franchise issue, Marthinus Steyn, the recently elected president of the Orange Free State, invited the two officials to Bloemfontein for face-to-face negotiations. Although unenthusiastic, Milner "could hardly refuse," author Byron Farwell observes.[11]

The Bloemfontein Conference lasted for just six days, from May 31 to June 5, 1899. From the start of the meeting, Milner insisted he would accept nothing less than a reduction in the Transvaal's residency requirements from the current 14 years to five years. After the talks had dragged on for nearly a week, Kruger made what he viewed as a major concession: He offered to approach the Volksraad regarding cutting the residency requirement in half, to just seven years. Milner, having already announced that he was pulling out of the talks, rejected Kruger's conciliatory gesture. "It is our country you want!" Kruger bitterly complained to the high commissioner.[12] Events of the next few months would lend a great deal of credence to his accusation.

# The Descent
# into War

The weeks immediately following the failed Bloemfontein Conference were tense, as Chamberlain and Milner
sought to build popular support for an African war among
British nationals at home and abroad. In mid-June 1899,
Chamberlain published an inflammatory telegram from Milner about the supposedly intolerable plight of the uitlanders.
In it, he compared their treatment by the Boers to that of the
*helots* (state-owned slaves of ancient Greece) by their Spartan
masters. In his "Helot Dispatch," as the telegram came to be
known, Milner contended that British diplomacy had accom-
plished all it could for the uitlanders. In his opinion, London
now had no choice but to intervene militarily on behalf of its
oppressed subjects. "It is idle to talk of peace and unity," the
high commissioner insisted.

> The case for intervention is overwhelming. . . . The spec-
> tacle of thousands of British subjects kept permanently in
> the position of helots . . . calling vainly to Her Majesty's
> Government for redress, steadily undermine the influence
> and reputation of Great Britain and the respect for the
> British Government within its own dominions.[1]

## KEEPING THE CRISIS AT A FEVER PITCH

Milner's "dramatic dispatch created a sensation, and not just in Britain," writes Byron Farwell. "The British in South Africa reacted as well. Throughout the winter months in South Africa—June, July, and August—there were anti-Boer demonstrations, public meetings, petitions, and incidents of all kinds, not only in the Transvaal, but also in Natal and the Cape Colony." A week after the release of the Helot Dispatch, Chamberlain did his part to keep anti-Boer sentiment in England at a fever pitch by publicly declaring that it was Britain's "duty, not only to the uitlander, . . . but to our own prestige . . . to insist that the Transvaal falls in line with the other states in South Africa, and no longer menaces the peace and prosperity of the world."[2] Exactly how the Afrikaner republic, which at a little more than 110,000 square miles (177,000 km) was roughly the size of the state of Arizona, was menacing "the peace and prosperity of the world," the colonial secretary did not explain.

At the same time that Milner, Chamberlain, and their backers within the British government were rallying public opinion behind a military solution to the uitlander problem, 73-year-old Paul Kruger was still trying to strike a bargain with the British. In July, he managed to convince the nationalistic members of the Volksraad into lowering the residency requirement for enfranchisement to seven years. Despite his suspicions regarding Britain's true intentions toward his country, Kruger could not believe that the English would risk another war over a mere two years—seven years for enfranchisement instead of five. He was wrong. Determined to keep the international crisis he had worked so hard to promote at the boiling point, Milner adamantly stuck to his earlier demand for full voting rights after five years' residency.

In late August, Jan Smuts, the Transvaal's young state attorney, approached British officials in southern Africa with a new offer: The Volksraad would reduce the residency requirement to five years on the condition that Britain refrained from interfering in the Transvaal's internal affairs in the future. But Pretoria's willingness to finally meet British terms for the franchise had come too late. After Kruger convinced the Volkstaad to lower the residency requirement to seven years, Milner and Chamberlain immediately began to downplay the franchise issue, focusing their attention instead on the much larger question of British supremacy in southern Africa. Fifteen years earlier, Kruger had talked Prime Minister Gladstone into removing all references to imperial suzerainty over his country from the London Convention, the revised peace settlement for the Transvaal War. Nevertheless, Milner, Chamberlain, and their supporters in the British government, including the prime minister himself, Lord Salisbury, insisted that just because the phrase was missing from the London Convention did not mean that imperial suzerainty over the Transvaal had ended in 1884. As a consequence of the British Empire's continuing status as the "paramount power in South Africa," they argued, it was not only Britain's right—but its solemn obligation—to oversee the internal and foreign affairs of both Boer republics.[3] Thus Pretoria's demand that Britain stay out of the republic's domestic affairs in the future, they declared, was completely unacceptable.

## THE BOERS ISSUE AN ULTIMATUM

Soon after the British government rejected Smuts's compromise proposal, Chamberlain asked his fellow Cabinet members to significantly increase the number of imperial troops in southern Africa. Unless the rebellious Boers were brought under control, he warned, the empire's standing in the region would be placed in grave doubt and with it "the estimate formed of our power and influence in our Colonies and throughout the world."[4] Lord Salisbury put it more bluntly. "The real point to be made to South Africa," the prime minister declared, "is that we, not the Dutch [Boers], are the Boss."[5] On September 8, the Cabinet, persuaded by Chamberlain's and Salisbury's arguments, voted unanimously to double the number of British troops in southern Africa by transferring 10,000 soldiers from imperial garrisons in India and the Mediterranean basin to the region. In response to the Cabinet's resolution, worried uitlanders began fleeing Johannesburg by the trainload, most of them heading for the British colonies of Natal and the Cape.

By this point, Kruger and most other Boer leaders, including President M.T. Steyn of the Orange Free State, had reconciled themselves to the idea of war with Britain. If they failed to stand up to the British, they believed, both Boer republics would soon be reduced to the status of crown colonies. Through September, as the 10,000 British reinforcements began arriving in southern Africa, Kruger and Steyn continued to construct new forts and import the most up-to-date German and French small arms and artillery. By the beginning of October, the two states had mobilized their commando forces. "The Lord will protect us," Kruger assured a nervous Volksraad. "The Lord gave us the triumph of the War of Independence [the Transvaal War] and the capture of Jameson. The Lord will also protect you now, even if thousands of bullets fly about you."[6]

On October 9, shortly after government officials finally agreed to mobilize troops in the British Isles for a possible war in southern Africa, Kruger and Steyn issued a joint ultimatum to London. They declared that London must recall the thousands of reinforcements sent to southern Africa and remove all imperial troops from the Transvaal borders within the next 48 hours, or they would consider their states to be at war with Britain. As both men fully expected, the British government promptly rejected their uncompromising demands. At 5:00 P.M. on October 11, 1899, the Transvaal and Orange Free State officially declared war on Great Britain. Although Chamberlain had been quietly drafting an ultimatum of his own, he was thrilled that Kruger and Steyn had beaten him to the punch. "They have done it!" the colonial secretary exclaimed when informed of the Boer ultimatum. By acting first, Chamberlain observed, the Afrikaner republics had cast themselves as the aggressors in the conflict and conveniently "liberated" his government "from the necessity of explaining to the people of England why we were at war."[7]

## THE BOERS TAKE THE INITIATIVE

Until British expeditionary forces arrived in southern Africa from England, Kruger and Steyn realized, the Boers, with a combined commando force of more than 50,000, possessed a significant numerical advantage over their enemy. Determined to strike quickly, the Afrikaners immediately launched a bold offensive into the British colonies.

The main thrust of the Boer offensive was to extend deep into Natal, where most of the imperial troops in South Africa were then concentrated. While one group of commandos laid siege to Ladysmith, the colony's second-largest town and the site of a major British garrison, another was to fight its way south to the vital coastal port of Durban, the anticipated landing spot for the English expeditionary army. Simultaneously, a second arm of the offensive would push into the Cape Colony from the Orange Free State. This arm had several goals: sever the rail line linking the colony with Rhodesia; capture the major mining city of Kimberley (which, along with the rest of Griqualand West, had been annexed by the Cape in 1880); and isolate the railway junction and garrison at Mafeking, along the border with British Bechuanaland.

By early November, commando forces occupied much of northern Natal and had successfully invested Mafeking,

This November 1899 illustration taken from the French publication *Le Petit Journal* shows inhabitants fleeing Ladysmith, the colony's second-largest city and the location of an important British garrison, during the Boer War.

Kimberley, and Ladysmith, trapping 1,000, 2,600, and 13,700 British troops, respectively, in the three towns. (In military terminology, "investment" means surrounding an enemy town or fort with armed forces to block entry or escape.) Nonetheless, if the first several weeks of fighting had proved a near disaster for the British, the tide of war was about to turn in their favor. On October 31, General Sir Redvers Buller, the new commander-in-chief of British forces in southern Africa, had arrived at Cape Town accompanied by tens of thousands of troops from the British Isles. Several other troopships soon followed. By November 15, the British expeditionary army in South Africa, the 1st Army Corps, had swelled to 47,000 soldiers, including 38 infantry battalions and seven cavalry regiments.

## BULLER DEVELOPS A PLAN

Upon landing at Cape Town, Buller learned that Ladysmith, Kimberley, and Mafeking were under siege and Boer troops occupied most of northern Natal as well as parts of the northern Cape. Buller immediately scrapped his original plans for a major offensive thrust up the railway line linking Cape Town to the Free State capital of Bloemfontein and Pretoria. Instead, he resolved to drive all Boer troops out of northern Natal and relieve Ladysmith and Kimberley as soon as possible. To achieve these objectives, he divided his force into several parts. The largest of the forces, under his command, had the task of pushing the Boers out of northern Natal and retaking the garrison at Ladysmith.

Throughout most of the month of November, as the imperial forces reorganized in preparation for Buller's new offensive, and the Boers devoted much of their precious resources to besieging the three British towns, there was little action of note in the war, with one exception. On November 15, near the town of Chieveley in Natal, Boer commandos ambushed an armored train that happened to be carrying a

*(continues on page 52)*

# TECHNOLOGY AND THE BOER WAR

During the Boer War, both sides, but especially the Boers, made extensive use of some of the latest technological advances in weaponry design and communications. Because of the huge revenues generated by the Rand goldfields, the Boer governments were able to purchase the most up-to-date artillery and small arms from Germany, France, and—ironically—Britain during the years immediately preceding the war. ("Small arms" are firearms such as revolvers and rifles capable of being carried by an individual soldier.) In the realm of artillery, the Boers imported quick-firing, long-range French- and German-manufactured guns along with several automatic cannons nicknamed "pom-poms" (because of the sound they made when fired) from Britain. Because the lightweight pom-poms "could be taken into places into which other artillery could not go," notes Martin Evans, "by the end of the war, the British were using them as well."*

Prior to the Jameson Raid, Boer commandos had to furnish their own small arms. As late as 1895, most of the farmer-warriors were still using antiquated, single-shot rifles instead of more technologically advanced (and expensive) magazine-fed rifles. (A magazine is a compartment in or on a firearm in which cartridges are stored to be fed into the gun chamber.) But in the wake of the raid, and the fears it generated among the Boers regarding Britain's true intentions in South Africa, presidents Kruger and Steyn purchased tens of thousands of state-of-the-art firearms for their commando forces, the majority of them rapid-firing, high-velocity Mauser rifles from Germany. Like the British-manufactured Lee-Metford and Lee-Enfield rifles used by British troops during the war, the Mausers had five-cartridge magazines. Nevertheless, there was a key difference between the commandos' state-of-the-art Mausers and the rifles used by their British foes. Historian Byron Farwell notes:

> The magazine of the British rifles had to be loaded one cartridge at a time and the soldiers carried their bullets loose in ammunition pouches; the Boers carried their cartridges in clips, and a five-round clip could be inserted quickly by a push of the thumb. Thus, while a British soldier could fire five rounds as fast as a Boer [commando], the latter could fire 50 rounds faster than the soldier could fire twenty because of the speed at which he could reload.**

In the realm of communications, the British and Boers alike took advantage of some—but by no means all—of the technological advances of the last few decades. Although both sides still relied heavily on mounted dispatch riders to relay orders and intelligence, the heliograph played a significant role in their battlefield communications. First used by the British in the Anglo-Afghan War of 1878-1880, the heliograph consisted of two mirrors that were mounted on a tripod and used to flash signals by means of the sun's rays. Neither the Boers nor the British, however, made much use of either the electric telegraph or the recently invented telephone during the conflict. Their "use on the battlefield," observes Farwell, "was limited, commanders not understanding their full potentiality. Before the war was over, a wireless message had crossed the Atlantic, but none crossed the veld."***

---

\* Martin Marix Evans, **The Boer War: South Africa 1899-1902.** Oxford: Osprey Publishing, 1999, p. 11.
\*\* Farwell, **The Great Anglo-Boer War**, p. 43.
\*\*\* Ibid., p. 45.

*(continued from page 49)*
young British newspaper reporter by the name of Winston Churchill. Despite his noncombatant status as a war correspondent, Churchill, along with some 60 others on the train, was hauled off to a detention camp in Pretoria. A few weeks later the future British prime minister, who would successfully lead his nation through World War II (1939–1945), managed to escape his Boer captors, ultimately making his way out of the Transvaal by stowing away on a freight train.

## "BLACK WEEK"

In late November, British troops advanced into the northern Cape, near the Orange River, where in several brief but bloody engagements, they managed to get the better of the Boer commandos who had pushed into the region from the Free State. Then, during the second full week of December, the British army suffered three devastating defeats in rapid succession, the first two occurring in the Cape and the third in Natal. The first of the shattering "Black Week" defeats, as the battles would come to be collectively known, took place on December 10 at Stormberg, an important railway junction in the northeastern Cape. Mounted Boer commandos decimated a British infantry column sent to recapture the strategic junction, with 750 infantrymen (out of a total force of 2,700) killed, wounded, or captured. The very next day at Magersfontein ridge, about 16 miles (26 km) from Kimberley, two British infantry brigades tried to break through entrenched Boer sharpshooters armed with state-of-the art long-range rifles. After the brigades had sustained more than 900 casualties, the attack disintegrated in confusion, with the panicky troops fleeing the ridge under blistering enemy fire in a humiliating rout that cost even more British lives.

The low point of Black Week, however, came on December 15, near the village of Colenso along Natal's Tugela River. It involved the large 18,000-man force Buller had assembled to win back northern Natal and relieve Ladysmith. When the British general's troops approached the river, which blocked their advance to the besieged town, they found themselves under fire from several thousand Boer riflemen and artillerists, who had been lying in wait across the waterway from Colenso in the hills lining the Tugela's northern bank. Under the adept leadership of their commander, Louis Botha, a 37-year-old Transvaal farmer, the Afrikaner defenders repulsed every British attempt to cross the river. With casualties mounting, Buller ordered his troops to withdraw, leaving behind 10 of his 12 field guns and a number of wounded men to be captured by the enemy in the process. Just 38 of Botha's 7,000 commandos were killed or wounded during the fighting near the Tulega River on December 15. In sharp contrast, Buller's force had sustained more than 1,000 casualties by the end of the Battle of Colenso. Many English newspapers compared the loss to the humiliating British defeat at Majuba Hill by the Boers nearly two decades earlier.

## "WE ARE NOT INTERESTED IN THE POSSIBILITIES OF DEFEAT"

When the Transvaal and Orange Free State first declared war on Great Britain on October 11, most Britons had assumed that the little Afrikaner republics would be beaten by Christmas. Majuba, they believed, was finally about to be avenged. Reflecting the public's confident mood, the editors of the British magazine *Punch* published a cartoon of John Bull, a well-known personification of England, towering over his Boer adversaries. "As you will *fight*, you shall have it. *This* time it's a fight to the finish," Bull warned in the caption.[8] After the calamitous reverses of Black Week, however, the hopes of the British public and press for a quick and painless victory in South Africa were replaced by a sense of outrage and shame. Along with the ongoing Boer sieges of Ladysmith, Kimberley, and Mafeking,

*(continues on page 56)*

# BLACK AFRICANS AND THE SIEGE OF MAFEKING

Of the three sieges of British garrison towns in Natal and the Cape, the siege of Mafeking was the longest and the most famous. For 217 days, 1,000 British troops under the command of Colonel Robert Baden-Powell; 500 white, chiefly male townspeople (Baden-Powell had evacuated white children and most white women before the investment began); and some 5,000 African refugees from the neighboring all-black town of Mafeking, held out against their Boer besiegers. "The whole episode," notes Gregory Fremont-Barnes, "was cast as an epic of bravery and fortitude in the British Press," and the resolute and resourceful Baden-Powell, who would later go on to found the Boy Scout movement, "emerged as a national hero."*

Everyone trapped in Mafeking suffered during the lengthy siege as food supplies steadily dwindled. Nonetheless, the hardships endured by the thousands of black women, men, and children during the seven-month ordeal are incalculable. According to historian Peter Warwick, in addition to aiding in the defense of the town during the siege,

> black military assistance helped the besieged garrison in a variety of other ways. African work parties were requisitioned daily during the siege and were responsible for constructing all the town's defenses, sometimes under heavy fire from the Boers. . . . Baden-Powell's local intelligence was almost wholly based on the reports of black scouts and spies. . . . All the

information which reached the outside world about the plight of the town was carried through the Boer lines at night by black runners. . . .**

Despite the indispensable assistance that Mafeking's black inhabitants provided to Baden-Powell and his troops, however, garrison officials allocated fewer and less-nutritious rations to native Africans than those provided to white civilians as food stocks shrank. Three months into the siege, a sympathetic white townswoman, Ina Cowan, bemoaned the emaciated condition of some of the blacks. The Africans, she reported in her diary, "dig up dead horses and eat them, and sit and pick on the rubbish heaps. Some of them are starving. I have seen as many dreadful things as I ever wish to see." Solomon T. Plaatje, a young black native of South Africa who worked as the official interpreter at the Magistrate's Court in Mafeking and would become a distinguished author, politician, and journalist, was dismayed by the plight of the town's native African population. "It was a miserable scene," he confided in his diary, "to be surrounded by about 50 hungry beings, agitating the engagement of your pity and to see one of them succumb to his agonies and fall backwards with a dead thud." The exact number of blacks who succumbed to starvation or disease during the siege of Mafeking will never be known, but some scholars place the death toll at more than 1,000, with the majority of the victims being young children.***

* Fremont-Barnes, **The Boer War**, p. 53.
** Peter Warwick, **Black People and the South African War: 1899-1902**. Cambridge: Cambridge University Press, 1983, pp. 34-35.
*** Ibid., pp. 36-37.

Although the Boer War is remembered today as a battle between two white groups for domination over South Africa, black soldiers fought for both sides during the conflict. Seen here, black African farm workers who fought with the British during the war.

*(continued from page 53)*

"the triple disasters at Stormberg, Magersfontein, and Colenso," Fremont-Barnes writes, "were . . . a source of immense consternation in Britain. Incredulity gave way to the realization that a small number of farmers could inflict telling blows against the disciplined forces of the world's greatest empire."[9]

Stung by charges that the South African war had been mismanaged, British government officials removed Buller as commander in chief and replaced him with 67-year-old Field Marshal Frederick Roberts, one of the empire's most celebrated war heroes. (Roberts's own son, a lieutenant in the King's Royal Rifle Corps, had been fatally wounded during the fighting at Colenso on December 15.) To serve as Roberts's chief of staff and second in command, the British government recruited another war hero, General Lord Horatio Herbert Kitchener, commander of the Egyptian army since 1892. As Roberts and Kitchener set off for southern Africa, two more British army divisions, "the last readily available," according to historian Martin Meredith, were also being dispatched to the region.[10] "We are not interested in the possibilities of defeat. They do not exist," Queen Victoria declared.[11]

# The British
# Fight Back

The shocking battlefield losses of Black Week strengthened popular support for the British war effort, not only in England but in other parts of the British Empire as well. At home, tens of thousands of ordinary Britons signed up to help beat the Boers, including a large volunteer unit raised by the city of London and a nearly 20,000-strong volunteer cavalry regiment dubbed the Imperial Yeomanry. Many residents of the self-governing British colonies of Canada, Australia, and New Zealand were also eager to do their part to ensure a British victory. By the end of the conflict, 16,500 Australian volunteers, most of them mounted soldiers, had fought for the British along with nearly 8,500 Canadians and 6,500 New Zealanders—the latter a particularly impressive number for such a small country. Additional support was provided by thousands of volunteers from the Cape Colony and Natal as well as by uitlander refugees from Johannesburg. By mid-February, British forces in southern Africa had swelled to nearly 180,000, of which approximately 130,000 were British regulars, with the rest being volunteers.

## THE RELIEF OF KIMBERLEY AND THE BATTLE OF PAARDEBERG

After arriving in Cape Town in January 1900, the new British commander in chief for southern Africa, Lord Frederick Roberts, immediately began to prepare his massive army for a new offensive designed to end the Boers' long investment of Kimberley and drive them out of the northern Cape altogether. Roberts personally led the force of 37,000 soldiers, cavalry, and artillerists that was assembled to carry out the campaign.

On the evening of February 15, British troops successfully entered Kimberley, following a daring cavalry dash that took them right through the center of one of the Boers' main defensive positions near the Modder River. Among the more than 50,000 white civilians, regular and volunteer soldiers, and black servants and mine laborers who had been trapped in Kimberley when the siege began was Cecil Rhodes, the mining magnate and mastermind of the Jameson Raid. Over the course of the four-month siege, Rhodes's insistence on assuming a prominent role in organizing the city's defense had proven a major source of irritation for the garrison commander, Lieutenant Colonel Kekewich. When the Boers stepped up their bombardment of Kimberley in early February 1900, Rhodes sent circulars around the city exhorting women and children to seek refuge from the deadly artillery barrages in his diamond mines. Thousands of panicky citizens followed Rhodes's advice and went down into the mines, an action that undoubtedly kept the town's casualty rate lower than it would have been otherwise, but which also greatly complicated Kekewich's efforts to provide food and other essential supplies to Kimberley's civilian population.

In the wake of the relief of Kimberley, the main Boer commando force in the northern Cape, led by General Piet Cronje, retreated eastward into the Orange Free State. As the British closed in on them near Paardeberg, the Boers hastily formed their large convoy of wagons into a defensive circle and dug themselves in for a siege along the banks of the Modder River.

# GANDHI AND THE BOER WAR

The famous Indian nationalist leader, Mohandas Gandhi (1869–1948), also known as Mahatma Gandhi, came to South Africa from his homeland six years before the outbreak of the Boer War. In 1893, after earning a law degree in London and working briefly as a lawyer in Bombay, the 24-year-old Gandhi was hired by an Indian merchant company in Natal to assist it in its ongoing legal battle with another trading company based in Pretoria. While traveling to Pretoria from Natal with a first-class rail ticket, Gandhi was verbally and physically abused by several white Transvaalers, including one of the train's conductors, who refused to accept the presence of a "colored" man in a first-class compartment. Shocked and angered by this ugly incident, Gandhi vowed to work for greater political and civil rights for South Africa's Indian immigrants who, even in British-run Natal, were all too often treated as second-class citizens.

After spending a year in Pretoria, where Indians were forbidden from using public sidewalks and were placed under a strict nighttime curfew, Gandhi returned to Natal. There he helped found the Natal Indian Congress and took a leading role in the organization's crusade to convince

On February 17, British troops, commanded by Chief of Staff Lord Kitchener (Roberts had contracted influenza), began pounding the Boer commandos with artillery fire. The following morning, too impatient to bombard or starve the enemy into surrendering, Kitchener made the exact error that Buller and other British commanders had committed

British officials to grant greater political rights to the colony's Indian residents. When the Boer War erupted in 1899, Martin Meredith writes, "Gandhi saw an opportunity to impress on the British authorities the loyalty and value of the Indian population."* Along with several dozen members of the Natal Indian Congress, Gandhi volunteered to serve the British war effort in whatever way he was needed—excluding on the battlefield—declaring that it would be a privilege to serve the Queen and the Empire.

At first, British officials brushed off Gandhi's offer. Following the horrific casualties of Black Week in December 1899, however, when General Buller himself suggested that the Natal government recruit Indians as stretcher-bearers, the officials turned to the gifted young lawyer to help organize the new Indian ambulance corps. Eventually Gandhi helped recruit more than 1,000 volunteers for the Natal corps, which would serve with distinction at a number of battles, including Spion Kop. Following the end of the Boer War in 1902, Gandhi resumed his campaign for greater Indian rights in South Africa. In 1914, after spending two decades in South Africa, Gandhi returned to his homeland, where he soon became a leader in the Indian campaign for independence from British rule.

* Meredith, **Diamonds, Gold, and War**, p. 505.

# A FIRSTHAND ACCOUNT OF
# THE SIEGE OF KIMBERLEY

By the time that British troops managed to drive through the Boers' defensive positions around the mining center and to relieve Kimberley, nearly 1,700 of the besieged city's 50,000 men, women, and children had been killed by enemy artillery fire. On February 9, H.V. MacLennan, an employee of the city's waterworks, described the horrific final week of the siege, when the Boers stepped up their bombardment by opening fire on the city with a state-of-the-art cannon manufactured by the French armaments company, Creusot. Nicknamed the "Long Tom" for its nearly 14-foot-long (4.2-meter) gun barrel, the Creusot cannon had a striking range of 5.5 miles (9 km) and shells weighing over 90 pounds (40.6 kilograms). MacLennan wrote:

> We are having an awful time now. The Boers have a six inch [barrel diameter] gun firing into Kimberley from Kampusdam. . . . Saw a woman and child killed by a 100 pound shell. It was an awful sight. God help the first Boer I get in my power. The Boers have now killed poor Labram [George Labram, an engineer for Rhodes' mining company]. I was with him for two hours before he died. He just went upstairs to wash his hands and I stayed below. Bang went the gun. We all waited to hear the burst, when it struck the very hotel we were in. . . . I went outside to have a look at the damage, when I saw that it was Labram's room that had been struck. Poor chap he was in an awful mess. His head was nearly off. His heart was taken clean away and his left leg was just hanging on by a thread. . . . He was buried on Saturday night at 8 P.M. and the brutes of Boers shelled his funeral.*

* Quoted in Smurthwaite, **The Boer War**, p. 99.

Standing at center, Cecil Rhodes, the British imperialist, businessman, and mining magnate, with others during the Boer siege of Kimberley in February 1900. During the bombardment, Rhodes urged women and children to seek shelter in his diamond mines.

time and again over the past three months: He launched a frontal assault on the well-entrenched Boer riflemen. In the face of heavy and accurate enemy fire from their concealed foes, Kitchener's army had suffered more than 1,200 casualties by day's end, as opposed to just 300 for the Boers. On being informed of the horrific death toll at Paardeberg on February 18, Roberts firmly rejected Kitchener's proposal to renew the infantry assault. Cronje finally agreed to an unconditional surrender on February 27, following a week and a half of nonstop bombardment from British artillery guns. In what was the Afrikaners' most devastating defeat in the entire war, 4,000 Boer commandos were rounded up and exiled to remote prisoner-of-war camps in the West Indies, Ceylon, and the South Atlantic island of St. Helena.

## BULLER'S RENEWED CAMPAIGN TO RELIEVE LADYSMITH

After being appointed as the new commander in chief of British forces in South Africa, Roberts left his predecessor, General Buller, in charge of all military operations in Natal. In late January, a little more than a month after his defeat at Colenso, Buller tried again to break through Boer defenses at the Tugela River to relieve Ladysmith. Once again, his troops were repulsed by Louis Botha and his Boer sharpshooters several miles upstream from Colenso in the Battle of Spion Kop, at a cost of 1,500 British dead or wounded. On February 5, Buller launched yet another fruitless attempt to push through Botha's defenses at Vaal Krantz, just east of Spion Kop.

Beginning in mid-February, the tide began to turn for Buller in his two-month-long campaign to relieve Ladysmith. After breaking through the main Boer defensive position four miles (about 6.5 km) north of the Tugela, the first British troops entered Ladysmith on February 28, a day after Cronje's surrender at Paardeberg and 118 days after the siege began. By this time, nearly 600 of the 14,000 soldiers stuck in Ladysmith since October 30 had died—the vast majority from enteric fever (typhoid) brought on by contaminated water supplies. Another 3,000 lay sick in the infirmary. In his diary, Private F.G. Tucker described the subdued welcome he and the other British troops who liberated Ladysmith on February 28 received from the garrison's sickly and emaciated defenders. "Instead of being cheered by all as we had imagined," he wrote, "most of them seemed to say with their looks: 'Well, you have come at last, but you have taken your time over it.'"[1]

British troops view the Boer position at Colenso in 1899. Following the British defeat at Colenso, General Redvers Buller sought to penetrate Boer defenses to relieve British troops at Ladysmith.

## ON TO BLOEMFONTEIN

With Kimberley and Ladysmith relieved at last, Roberts prepared in early March to take the war into the Orange Free State. Once he had secured the Free State capital at Bloemfontein, his plan was to press northward into the Transvaal and its capital city of Pretoria. On March 7, a commando force under General Christiaan de Wet failed to stop Roberts's much larger force from continuing their advance some 50 miles (80.5 km) west of Bloemfontein at Poplar Grove. On March 10, General Jacobus (Koos) de la Rey's commando group fought the British at Driefontein, but retreated when Roberts's troops moved to surround them. Vastly outnumbered by the enemy, the Free State's defenders realized there was no way they could stem the British tide. After Driefontein, Roberts and his men encountered no further resistance on the road to Bloemfontein. On March 13,

In this circa-1900 photo, Boer forces are seen in the field during the Boer War. Elusive, fast-moving Boers bedeviled the British with their devastating hit-and-run tactics.

they entered the capital "without firing a shot," according to author Fremont-Barnes.[2] President Steyn and his government had fled the city the day before for Kroonstad, about 130 miles (209 km) to the northeast.

Aside from the relief of Mafeking, Roberts believed all that now remained to assure a British victory was the capture of Pretoria. Yet he felt he could not push on to the Transvaal immediately. He needed time to reorganize his railroad transport system and replenish vital supplies. He also wanted to rest his weary troops, many of whom had come down with typhoid, possibly from drinking contaminated water during the siege of Paardeberg. In the end, Roberts and his men would linger for nearly two months in the Free State capital.

## THE BOERS RETHINK THEIR STRATEGY

While Roberts was resting, reorganizing, and restocking in Bloemfontein, Boer military and political leaders from the Transvaal and Orange Free State took advantage of this breathing space to organize a joint council of war at Kroonstad, the newly proclaimed capital of the Free State, in mid-March. The surrender of Cronje's large force at Paardeberg, the lifting of the sieges of Kimberley and Ladysmith, and the capture of Bloemfontein had "plunged the Boers' war effort into crisis," David Smurthwaite writes. "Morale plummeted . . . and the steady stream of men returning to their homes threatened to become a flood."[3]

Contributing to the Boers' declining morale in March 1900 was the realization that their hope of receiving military assistance from Germany, Holland, France, and other European nations sympathetic to their cause would probably remain unfulfilled. Since the war's outbreak, some 2,000 foreign volunteers had journeyed to South Africa from France, Italy, the United States, and other far-off countries to fight alongside the Boers. These volunteers were motivated by their ideals of liberty and national self-determination, a strong dislike for Great Britain, or merely a sense of adventure. Yet, even now, with the English seemingly on the verge of victory in South Africa, not a single foreign government had offered to intervene militarily on the Boers' behalf. "No nation was, in the last analysis, prepared to risk British retaliation against its own colonies for the sake of the Boers," Smurthwaite contends.[4]

On March 5, after Cronje's capture and the relief of Kimberley and Ladysmith, Kruger and Steyn sent a telegram to Lord Salisbury, offering to enter into peace negotiations immediately in return for the prime minister's guarantee of independence for their two countries. With victory in sight and nearly 13,000 British soldiers already killed or wounded since hostilities began in October 1899, however, London was in no

## "TOMMY ATKINS'S" DEADLIEST ENEMY

When the Boer War ended in May 1902, approximately 22,000 British troops had lost their lives. Of that number fully 13,000 had succumbed to disease. The deadliest enemy of Tommy Atkins (as the ordinary British soldier was nicknamed) was not the Boer rifleman, but rather typhoid, dysentery, and other contagious diseases.

David Smurthwaite writes, "The British soldier's exposure to sickness and disease began during the long, cramped and unhygienic voyage out to South Africa. . . . Some troopships disembarked units that were riddled with food poisoning, diarrhea and dysentery before they even set foot ashore." Thereafter, he observes, "difficulties of supply, the scarcity of fresh water on the veld, and nights spent lying awake soaked to the skin or freezing on top of a kopje [a small, isolated hill in the veld] were not calculated to keep soldiers healthy."*

Typhoid, the greatest scourge of the British army during the Boer War had been largely tamed throughout much of the world by the late nineteenth century, according to Thomas Pakenham. The medical community understood that "to prevent typhoid, you needed careful sanitation; to treat it, you needed careful nursing and a careful diet," he writes.** Unfortunately for Tommy Atkins, however, polluted mood to compromise. In his formal reply to Kruger and Steyn, Salisbury flatly rejected any possibility of self-rule for either of the Boer republics. On March 17, six days after Salisbury's rejection, Kruger and Steyn convened their joint council of war at Kroonstad.

---

drinking water sources, poor sanitary practices in army camps, and inadequate medical care and overcrowding in many field hospitals meant that the death rate among the British army from typhoid remained shockingly high throughout most of the Boer War.

During the height of the typhoid epidemic that swept through Bloemfontein, William Burdett-Coutts, a visiting British member of Parliament, was horrified by the conditions he encountered in a local field hospital, later recalling that

> hundreds of men . . . were lying in the worst stages of typhoid, with only a blanket and a thin waterproof sheet (not even the latter for many of them) between their aching bodies and the hard ground, with no milk and hardly any medicines, without beds, stretchers or mattresses, without linen of any kind, without a single nurse amongst them, with only a few ordinary private soldiers to act as "orderlies" . . . and with only three doctors to attend on 350 patients. . . . In many of these tents there were ten typhoid cases lying closely packed together, the dying with the convalescent, the man in his "crisis" pressed against the man hastening to it. There was no room to step between them. . . .[***]

---

* Smurthwaite, **The Boer War**, p. 122.
** Pakenham, **The Boer War**, p. 402.
*** Ibid., p. 403.

Quickly ruling out surrender as an option, the 50 political leaders and senior military officers who attended the council devoted themselves to rethinking the republics' military strategy. The council concluded that to move forward, all Boer commandos must be mounted and the use of slow-moving supply wagons be abandoned in order to increase their forces' mobility against their much more numerous enemy. At the urging of the Orange Free State's leading field general, Christiaan de Wet, they also determined to "tilt their defensive strategy progressively away from the conventional method of trying to block or delay an invasion by fighting at the front," Pakenham writes.[5] Instead, they would employ lightning-quick guerilla-style assaults on British communication lines, supply sources, and isolated garrisons or columns. De Wet and the rest of the Boer leaders at the Kroonstad meeting realized that an outright victory in the war was extremely unlikely at this point. Nonetheless, they hoped that if the commandos persisted with their destructive guerilla campaign long enough, the British would lose their will to fight and agree to a lenient peace settlement that allowed the republics to retain their independence.

At the end of March, de Wet launched the Boers' new guerilla strategy by mounting a lightning assault on Bloemfontein's sole source of fresh water, the waterworks at Sanna's Post, about 19 miles (30 km) from the city. When he heard that a large British wagon convoy had been spotted in the vicinity, however, he decided to ambush the supply convoy first and then secure the waterworks. On March 30, de Wet and a band of 400 mounted commandos staged a daring ambush on the British column, killing or wounding 150 and capturing 400 enemy troops, along with seven artillery guns, and large amounts of ammunition and food from the convoy's 92 ammunition carts and provisioning wagons. Returning to Sanna's Post, de Wet and his men were able to keep possession of the water pumps long enough to create a grave water shortage in Bloemfontein, worsening the typhoid epidemic that had already sickened thousands of Roberts's men.

## PRETORIA AND MAFEKING

Roberts and the rest of the British military leadership believed de Wet's attack on Sanna's Post and an April 4 assault on a British supply convoy at Reddersburg (during which the Boer general took more than 500 prisoners) to be no more than minor setbacks on the road to victory. Never imagining that de Wet's actions were the forerunners of a bold new strategy, they continued to assume that once the Transvaal, and particularly its capital, Pretoria, was under their control, the war would be over.

On May 3, seven weeks after he entered Bloemfontein, Roberts finally decided that his army was ready to resume its advance into the heart of Boer country. As he began to move on the Transvaal's two chief cities, Johannesburg and Pretoria, Roberts had nearly 200,000 troops at his disposal, while the Boers' combined forces had dwindled to an estimated 30,000 men. With the overwhelmed Boer commandos retreating rapidly before Roberts's "steamroller army," Kruger decided to abandon Pretoria and relocate his government in the remote grasslands of the eastern Transvaal.[6] On May 31, one day after Kruger departed Pretoria, Roberts's troops took control of Johannesburg, approximately 35 miles (56 km) south of the Transvaal capital. On June 5, they marched triumphantly into Pretoria without firing a shot, the commander in chief of the Transvaal forces, Louis Botha, having decided against defending the city.

While Roberts was advancing on Johannesburg and Pretoria, a British relief column under Colonel B.T. Mahon was heading toward the remote railroad junction and garrison town of Mafeking in the Cape Colony's northern tip. On May 12, as Mahon's men closed in on the British outpost, Mafeking's Boer besiegers made one last desperate effort to capture the town.

The garrison's commander, Colonel Baden-Powell, successfully repulsed the assault with the indispensable assistance of the town's large African population. Early on the morning of May 17, the first British troops entered Mafeking, finally bringing the seven-month-long siege to an end.

On June 11–12, Roberts's troops clashed with a commando force under Louis Botha at Diamond Hill, just east of Pretoria in the Transvaal, in what would turn out to be one of the last two formal battles of the conflict. In the end, Botha's men were forced to retreat, but their ability to hold their own against a much larger British army for two days brought new confidence and determination to the Boer military leadership. Two and a half months later, Boer and the British forces confronted one another in what would turn out to be the final conventional battle of the Boer War at Bergendal, near Machadodorp, the remote eastern Transvaal town where Kruger had established his new capital after fleeing Pretoria. As it had at Diamond Hill, the battle ended in victory for the bigger British force. By late August, Roberts's forces had captured Machadodorp (these did not include Kruger's forces, as he had already fled the town for Nelspruit, near the Mozambique border). As far as Roberts was concerned, the Boer War was all but won.

Yet neither the occupation of Machadodorp nor Roberts's victory proclamation on September 1 were destined to bring the conflict to an end. Although Roberts could not have imagined it at the time, the war was about to enter a new phase that would prove to be longer and, in many ways, far more challenging for the British than its first 11 months had proven.

# Kitchener Takes Drastic Measures

**B**y September 1900, most Boer leaders concurred that waging a no-holds-barred guerilla campaign against the British was their only chance of keeping the conflict alive. By ambushing isolated imperial units and destroying lines of communications in the occupied Transvaal and Orange Free State (officially renamed the Orange River by the British), as well as by launching raids into border areas of the Cape and Natal, they hoped to exhaust their enemy's resolve to fight. As British casualties and financial costs mounted with no end in sight, the Boer leaders reasoned, London would eventually conclude that retaining control over the Afrikaner republics was not worth the effort.

## THE EXPANDING GUERILLA WAR

To adopt the Boer commando system to the new, unconventional warfare, Boer generals—most notably the Transvaal's Botha, de la Rey, Smuts, and the Free State's de Wet—cast off artillery guns and other heavy equipment along with all encumbering baggage. Reorganized into small, highly mobile mounted units under the energetic direction of these commanders, the guerilla fighters devoted themselves to harassing and hindering the British occupying forces at every turn. As part of their new hit-and-run strategy, Boer commandos attacked detached columns and garrisons; dynamited bridges; cut telegraph wires; and sabotaged the railway lines on which the British depended to transport ammunition, food, and other essential supplies.

From the start, the fast-moving Boer raiders proved remarkably elusive, to the enormous frustration of Roberts and the rest of the British high command in South Africa. The guerilla commandos, or "bitter-enders," as those Boers who refused to relinquish the fight for an independent Free State and Transvaal following Pretoria's fall were popularly known, probably numbered no more than 25,000 in late 1900—just one-tenth the size of the British forces in South Africa. Yet, because of the vast geographical area over which the commandos ranged—an area larger than Germany and France combined—and their intimate knowledge of the terrain, the British found tracking down the commandos all but impossible. The army's dilemma was well illustrated by their struggle to corner perhaps the most successful of the commando generals, Christiaan de Wet. Although some 30,000 British troops pursued de Wet through the Free State and into the Transvaal during the last four months of 1900, the Boer leader outmaneuvered his would-be captors, eventually making his way across the Orange River to the Cape Colony in early 1901. For six weeks, de Wet led British cavalry troops on a wild chase through the rugged terrain of the eastern Cape, where he attempted to provoke rebellion among the area's largely Boer inhabitants before slipping back into the Free State in March.

As the de Wet fiasco made all too clear, the British high command was woefully unprepared for the unconventional warfare at which the Boer general and his fellow bitter-enders were rapidly becoming experts. "Short of mounted troops, scouts and intelligence," writes Martin Meredith, Roberts's forces "lumbered about the countryside in large numbers but with little effect."[1] The chief problem confronting Roberts and Lord Kitchener (Roberts's successor as British commander in chief after November 1900) as the Boer War entered its guerilla phase was that "their troops controlled only the ground on which they stood," David Smurthwaite observes. "As garrisons were based principally in the towns of the [former] Republics, this was where control could be imposed. In the vast spaces of the veld the occupation was as fleeting as the [British] columns which moved across it in search of the Boer commandos," Smurthwaite contends.[2]

During his last months in South Africa, Roberts attempted to quash the guerilla movement by using a carrot-and-stick approach. On the one hand, he generously offered amnesty for commandos who turned in their weapons and took an oath of neutrality. On the other, he sought to scare the Boers into submission by proclaiming that the British would retaliate for commando raids by destroying all Boer farms in the immediate vicinity of the attacks. Neither of Roberts's proclamations, however, had any noticeable impact on the Boers' destructive campaign against the British. By November 29, when Roberts officially relinquished his command to Kitchener, the field marshal had been compelled to deploy 45,000 troops along railway lines and at detached garrisons in the Orange River and Transvaal colonies in response to commando attacks.

## BLOCKHOUSES AND BARBED WIRE

When Roberts set sail for London in early December 1900, he believed, like most British military and political leaders, that the Boers were essentially beaten. He was confident that Kitchener would soon bring the troublesome bitter-enders to heel. After all, in his role as commander in chief of the Egyptian army, Kitchener had already shown himself to be not only a resourceful but also an extraordinarily ruthless military leader.

Kitchener recognized that the central factor behind the imperial army's dismal record against the commandos was the large size of the war zone and the ease with which the guerilla fighters could disappear into its seemingly endless grasslands. Determined to impede the commandos' mobility as much as possible, he devised an elaborate counter-tactic. Kitchener ordered the construction of a series of blockhouses (small forts) and barbed-wire barricades in areas frequented by commandos or likely to attract future guerilla attacks. Through his block-house scheme, Kitchener wanted to not only discourage future hit-and-run raids against British targets but also hoped to use the forts and long stretches of barbed wire that looped them together to ensnare the elusive guerillas. With that in mind, Kitchener organized tens of thousands of his finest cavalry and infantry units into big, fast-moving columns. These mobile columns were to conduct regular, coordinated sweeps across the veld, hopefully driving any raiding parties in their vicinity against his net of blockhouses and fences, where the trapped commandos could then be rapidly overwhelmed and captured.

During the early stages of the guerilla campaign, Lord Roberts had ordered the construction of a chain of two-story stone blockhouses along the Cape Town–Bloemfontein railroad to safeguard the army's chief supply line in South Africa. Roberts's substantial stone structures were not only costly but also very time-consuming to build, typically tak-ing a full three months to complete. This was unacceptable to Kitchener, since his strategy of using long lines of blockhouses to hem in and ensnare Boer raiders required thousands of the forts. Consequently, in late 1900, the new commander in chief called on the army engineering corps to design a less expen-sive and easier-to-fabricate structure than Roberts's massive dynamite-proof model. The engineers did not let Kitchener down. Made of double-skinned corrugated iron walls, separated by layers of rubble, and surrounded by deep trenches and wire entanglements on which tin cans were often hung as primitive alarms against intruders, these bullet-proof block-houses could be thrown up in less than a day by a half-dozen men. The first of the new blockhouses were erected in the Transvaal in January 1901. By the war's end 17 months later, 8,000 of the inexpensive yet solidly made forts, each of which could hold up to seven men, snaked across huge swathes of the Boer countryside, along with 4,000 miles (6,437 km) of barbed-wire fencing.

## KITCHENER'S "SCORCHED-EARTH" POLICY

Eventually, Kitchener's efforts to pen in the Boers would pay off handsomely, as his expanding network of blockhouses and fences began to seriously hamper the effectiveness and range of the guerilla units. Yet it took many months to put his elaborate enclosure system in place. In some areas, such as the western Transvaal, Bill Nasson writes, "tricky terrain, troublesome water shortages, and communication obstacles," prevented Kitchener from fully implementing his blockhouse strategy.[3] Consequently, soon after taking charge of the British war effort, Kitchener resolved to add a second major element to his anti-guerilla campaign. He decided to systematically destroy the Boer farming communities on which the commando raid-ers depended for food, shelter, fresh horses, and intelligence regarding British troop movements.

Before stepping down as commander in chief of British forces in South Africa, Roberts had ordered the retaliatory burning of Boer homes and farms within a several-mile radius of guerilla attacks. Determined to isolate the Boer raiders from any form of support on the veld, Kitchener decided to apply Roberts's punitive tactic "on a much larger scale, employing a full-scale scorched-earth policy intended to lay waste to all Boer farmsteads within the reach of his forces," Fremont-Barnes notes.[4] The enormous scope of the devastation wrought

Perhaps the most controversial aspect of the Boer War was the British attacks on civilians. Pictured here, British troops set fire to a Boer farmhouse during the conflict to keep it from becoming a safe haven for Boer fighters.

by Kitchener's ruthless new policy encompassed large sections of the Orange River and Transvaal colonies and even reached into Boer communities along the northern and eastern borders of the Cape Colony. As part of Kitchener's systemic campaign against the Boer civilian population, British troops destroyed acre upon acre of food crops, confiscated or slaughtered untold numbers of livestock, and torched an estimated 30,000 farmhouses and outbuildings.

In a letter, British Captain L. March Phillips vividly described the cruel toll Kitchener's scorched-earth strategy took on ordinary Boer families and revealed his own profound discomfort with the harsh policy:

> I had to go myself the other day, at the General's bidding,
> to burn a farm near the line of march. We got to the place
> and I gave the inmates, three women and some children,

ten minutes to clear their clothes and things out of the house, and my men then fetched bundles of straw and we proceeded to burn it down. The old grandmother was very angry. . . . Most of them, however, were too miserable to curse. The women cried and the children stood by holding on to them and looking with large frightened eyes at the burning house. . . . We rode away and left them, a forlorn little group, standing among their household goods—beds, furniture, and gimcracks strewn about the veldt; the crackling of the fire in their ears, and smoke and flame streaming overhead. The worst moment is when you first come to the house. The people thought we had called for refreshments, and one of the women went to get milk. Then we had to tell them that we had come to burn the place down. I simply didn't know which way to look. . . .[5]

Later in the letter, Phillips described an unforgettable act of defiance by a Boer child whose home had been targeted for destruction:

At another farm a small girl interrupted her preparation for departure to play indignantly their national anthem at us on an old piano. We were carting people off. It was raining hard and blowing—a miserable, hurried home-leaving; ransacked house, muddy soldiers, a distracted mother saving one or two trifles and pushing along her children to the ox-wagon outside, and this poor little wretch in the midst of it pulling herself to strum a final defiance.[6]

## CONCENTRATION CAMPS

Kitchener's scorched-earth policy quickly gave rise to a serious refugee problem in the Orange River and Transvaal colonies. Under Roberts, the army had established primitive tent camps for displaced Boer families. Kitchener greatly increased the number and size of these makeshift refugee centers, particularly from early 1901 on, when he decided that all civilians from "hostile districts"—areas that had persistently sheltered and provided intelligence to commandos—should be rounded up and sent to the temporary settlements, by force if necessary.[7] "Thus the nature of the camps changed; henceforth they were to hold the willing and the unwilling," Farwell observes.[8] In time, the continually expanding tent cities would come to be known as concentration camps, after the civilian detention or "reconcentration" camps used by Spain during the Cuban Insurrection of 1895–1898 to deprive the insurrectionists of civilian support.

By the end of the Boer War, 109 concentration camps in the former Boer republics held hundreds of thousand of internees. Forty-five were for whites; 64 for black Africans. Unlike the white camps, whose inmates were overwhelmingly women and children—most of them relatives of commandos—black camps also contained a number of men. Some were servants or other employees of Boer detainees or commandos. Others were farmers and herders whose crop stores and cattle had been destroyed by the British army on the suspicion that Boer guerilla bands had been confiscating livestock and foodstuffs from them. Most were put to work by the British army, growing food for the refugee camps, building fortifications, and performing a variety of other tasks.

Although conditions were particularly poor in the black camps, all of the concentration camps were overcrowded, unsanitary, and chronically short on food, particularly fresh vegetables and milk. Major disease outbreaks were the inevitable result of contaminated water supplies, meager rations, closely placed tents, and inadequate medical facilities. By mid-1902, at least 20,000 black Africans and up to 28,000 Boers had died in the makeshift camps, the vast majority from contagious diseases such as typhoid, measles, and dysentery. Nearly 80 percent of the Afrikaner dead were children under the age of 16. "More Boer boys and girls died in British concentration

Another very controversial British policy during the Boer War was the imprisonment of Boer families in concentration camps. This was the first use of civilian internment during wartime. Seen here, one such camp in 1900.

camps than all the fighting men killed by bullets and shells on both sides in the course of the entire war," Farwell notes.[9]

## A GROWING CONTROVERSY

Back in England, rumors of the appalling conditions in the Boer concentration camps soon made their way to Parliament. In January 1901, the Conservative war minister, John Brodrick, cabled Kitchener to let him know that "pretty bad reports" about the large refugee camp at Bloemfontein had reached Westminster and some Liberal Party members of Parliament were beginning to express concern. "I think I shall have a hot

*(continues on page 84)*

# EMILY HOBHOUSE, HUMAN RIGHTS ACTIVIST

The woman responsible for alerting the British public to the shocking conditions in South Africa's concentration camps was born into an Anglican clergyman's family in Cornwall, England. Until she was 35, Emily Hobhouse served as a companion and nurse to her widowed and sickly father. Following his death in 1895, she volunteered to go to the United States as an Anglican missionary. The Church of England sent Hobhouse to Virginia, Minnesota, where thousands of impoverished young men from her native Cornwall had emigrated to toil in the town's iron mines. Hobhouse remained for several years in Minnesota, preaching the benefits of temperance to Virginia's hard-drinking miners.

In late 1900, Hobhouse, now living in London, heard about the growing refugee problem in the Transvaal and Orange River colonies from a relative who held a seat in Parliament. Hobhouse then decided to travel to the Transvaal and Orange River colonies, where she planned to distribute donated clothes, blankets, and other supplies to the refugees. In January 1901, after receiving permission to tour the Bloemfontein concentration camp, she headed for the largest of the Orange River camps. At Bloemfontein, she found nearly 2,000 women and children packed together in fly-infested tents on the barren veld with "not a vestige of a tree in any direction, nor shade of any description."* Fuel, drinking water, nutritious food, clothing, and other basic necessities were in short supply, she noted, while the death rate from disease, particularly among the camp's youngest inmates, was shockingly high. The anguish of one Boer mother whose baby had fallen ill made a particularly deep impression on Hobhouse. "The mother," she later recalled,

> sat on her little trunk, with the child across her knee. She had nothing to give it and the child was sinking fast. . . . There was nothing to be done and we watched the child draw its last breath in reverent silence.
>
> The mother neither moved nor wept, it was her only child. Dry-eyed but deathly white she sat there motionless looking not at the child but far far away into the depths of grief beyond all tears. . . . The scene made an indelible impression on me.**

Over the next two months, Hobhouse visited five other concentration camps in the former Boer republics, where she encountered most of the same squalid conditions she had observed at Bloemfontein. In April, she returned to London, resolved to open her fellow Britons' eyes to the cruelty of Kitchener's policies. Although Hobhouse was publicly dismissed by government officials as a "pro-Boer" and a "screamer," her humanitarian crusade to bring attention to the plight of the Boer War's civilian victims aroused widespread public support in England, eventually prompting the British government to take important steps toward improving conditions in the camps.***

Hobhouse's humanitarian efforts on behalf of the Boer War's civilian victims continued even after the fighting was over. After the war's end in May 1902, she published a new exposé of the concentration camps, **The Brunt of the War and Where it Fell**, donating all royalties from the book's sales to help Boers whose farms had been destroyed.

---

\* Quoted in Meredith, **Diamonds, Gold, and War**, p. 455.
\*\* Quoted in Fremont-Barnes, **The Boer War**, p. 80.
\*\*\* Quoted in Pakenham, **The Boer War**, p. 532.

*(continued from page 81)*

time over these probably in most cases inevitable sufferings or privations," Brodrick wrote, asking Kitchener for a detailed account of camp conditions to help defend himself against his Liberal critics. Kitchener cabled back that reports of insufficient food, fresh water, clothing, and medical care had been greatly exaggerated and that the internees were "happy" and well cared for.[10]

Until the spring of 1901, the British public remained largely unaware of the controversy regarding the South African internment centers. The woman who finally brought the camps' appalling conditions to the attention of ordinary Britons was Emily Hobhouse, a 41-year-old humanitarian reformer, pacifist, and former missionary. In early 1901, Hobhouse made the long journey from London to Cape Town to distribute donated clothing and other supplies to Boer women and children left homeless by the war. From late January until early April 1901, Hobhouse traveled through the Orange River and Transvaal colonies, visiting a half-dozen Boer concentration camps along her way. Dismayed by the internment centers' horrific sanitation and medical facilities; high death rates; and chronic shortages of fuel, fresh water, and other necessities, she sailed home in May determined to expose the camps' squalid conditions to her fellow Britons.

Shortly after returning to London in the late spring of 1901, Hobhouse published a detailed account of the overcrowded and unhealthy camps she had toured in South Africa, particularly stressing the suffering of the camps' youngest inmates. Just as she had hoped, the British press and public were outraged by Kitchener's callous policies toward Boer civilians and demanded that the government take immediate action to reform the poorly run camps. Spurred on by the popular response to Hobhouse's exposé, many Liberal politicians enthusiastically championed her cause. David Lloyd George, MP, even went so far as to accuse the British army of pursuing

The British humanitarian Emily Hobhouse served as secretary of the South Africa Conciliation Committee and brought attention to the horrific conditions she found in British concentration camps in South Africa.

what amounted to a "policy of extermination" against women and children. "When children are being treated in this way and dying, we are simply ranging the deepest passions of the human heart against British rule in Africa," he contended.[11]

Although Minister of War Brodrick publicly dismissed the Liberal MPs' attacks on the internment centers as politically motivated, he and his fellow cabinet members were deeply concerned about the escalating public outcry over the camps. By the end of the summer, the British government had taken several significant and well-publicized steps to improve conditions and reduce death rates in the controversial tent cities. These included placing the camps under civilian control, allocating additional government funds for food and other basic necessities for inmates, and sending an all-female commission to South Africa under the direction of suffragist Millicent Garrett Fawcett to conduct a thorough investigation of the internment centers. The Fawcett Commission's report on the nearly two-dozen Boer concentration camps they visited not only confirmed Hobhouse's earlier findings but also echoed most of her recommendations for reforming the centers, including a complete overhaul of their sanitary and medical facilities. By the late winter of 1902, implementation of the commission's recommendations had led to a dramatic decline in the monthly death rate within the white concentration camps, from more than 20 percent to just 2 percent. Extensive dietary and sanitation reforms were also introduced in black concentration camps, resulting in significantly reduced mortality rates among native African internees as well.

In early 1902, Kitchener decided to change his tactics regarding Boer families displaced by his scorched-earth policy. No more civilians, he ordered his column commanders, were to be shipped off to the already overcrowded concentration camps. "Viewed as a gesture to the Liberals," writes Thomas Pakenham, Kitchener's new policy "was a shrewd political move." Yet leaving destitute Boer women and children to their own devices on the veld also "made excellent military sense," Pakenham observes, since, as Kitchener well knew, the responsibility of protecting and caring for them would now fall on the already overburdened Boer leadership.[12] The plight of the homeless women and children, who soon numbered in the thousands, deeply worried their commando relations in the field. It would also play an important part in the bitter-enders' willingness to finally engage in peace talks with their British opponents in April 1902, nearly two years after the fall of Pretoria.

# The Peace of Vereeniging

In early April 1902, leaders from the two former Boer republics, including President Steyn and generals de Wet, de la Rey, Botha, and Smuts, gathered at Klerksdorp in the southern Transvaal to discuss whether to begin serious negotiations with the British. Representing the Transvaal government was the republic's acting president, Schalk Burger; Paul Kruger, exhausted by the imperial army's relentless pursuit after the fall of Pretoria, had fled South Africa for Europe in October 1900. On April 11, two and a half years to the day after the Transvaal and Orange Free State declared war on Great Britain, a 10-man Boer delegation led by Burger departed Klerksdorp for Kitchener's Pretoria headquarters. They carried with them a blueprint for a peace settlement with their longtime foe.

# THE DECLINE OF THE BOER FORCES

The willingness of Steyn, de Wet, and others to initiate peace talks with the British was directly linked to the sorry state of the Afrikaners' armed forces. By early 1902, the Boer military machine was rapidly losing strength and resources. Kitchener's ever-expanding scorched-earth and encirclement campaigns in the Transvaal and Orange River colonies had exacted a terrible toll from the commandos, leaving many units exhausted and on the brink of starvation.

As the Boer War dragged into its third year, commandos endured shortages of food, clothing, medicine, ammunition, and other essential supplies. Deneys Reitz, a member of General Smuts's guerilla unit, was horrified by the disheveled appearance of a group of 300 commandos he encountered from the particularly hard-hit eastern Transvaal in April 1902. The "starving, ragged men, clad in skins or sacking, their bodies covered with sores, from lack of salt or food had reached the limits of physical endurance," he was convinced.[1] Many bitter-enders were under great emotional as well as physical strain as the war ground on with no end in sight. The plight of loved ones languishing in British internment centers, or even more distressing, wandering unprotected about the veld following Kitchener's decision to seal off the camps to new inmates, weighed heavily on the commandos, causing their already dwindling morale to plummet further.

It was not only the morale of the Boer forces that was dwindling during the first months of 1902; their numbers were also steadily declining. Two and a half years after the first shots of the war were fired, the number of commandos in the field had fallen dramatically. At least 7,000 Boer combatants out of an original force of approximately 52,000 were dead. A whopping 30,000 had been captured by the British and packed off to remote prison camps, some as far away as India or the Caribbean. Thousands of other commandos, derisively dubbed "hands-uppers," had voluntarily surrendered to British rule in return for amnesty. By April, as many as 4,000 of the surrendered commandos had become "joiners," as the bitter-enders called former comrades in arms who collaborated with the British. Convinced that defeat

# DENEYS REITZ, A YOUNG BOER COMMANDO

When the Boer War erupted in October 1899, Deneys Reitz was 17 years old and the son of a high-ranking Transvaal official. An ardent Boer nationalist, he immediately headed for the Natal border with the nearly 300 other members of his Pretoria commando. Until the very last day of the Boer War on May 31, 1902, young Reitz would remain a commando, taking part in some of the conflict's most famous battles, including the bloody Battle of Spion Kop. During the war's long guerilla phase, Reitz served first under Christiaan de Wet in the Transvaal, and later under Jan Smuts, accompanying the commando general on his final effort to incite rebellion among the Cape's Boer population in September and October of 1901. Journeying through the rugged terrain of the eastern Cape, Smuts and his 250 handpicked commandos skirmished repeatedly with enemy patrols and endured week after week of driving rains and penetrating cold.

In 1929, Reitz published a best-selling account of his war experiences entitled **Commando: A Boer Journal of the Boer War**. In his memoirs, Reitz described in vivid detail the hardships he faced as a guerilla fighter, including the grueling six weeks he spent with Smuts in the mountains of the eastern Cape in late 1901. "By day we were wet and was inevitable and anxious to stop the fighting so that they and their families could start to rebuild their shattered lives, joiners assisted the imperial army in many different capacities, including as scouts, guides, spies, and even armed combatants.

cold, and the nights were evil dreams," Reitz recalled. "Dry fuel was almost unprocurable, and after a weary day we had to spend the hours of darkness cowering together to snatch a little sleep on some muddy mountainside, or in an equally sodden valley." On one particularly cold and stormy night, he wrote:

> Our guide lost his way; we went floundering ankle-deep in mud and water, our poor, weakened horses stumbling and slipping at every turn; the rain beat down on us, and the cold was awful. Towards midnight it began to sleet. The grain-bag which I wore froze solid on my body, like a coat of mail, and I believe that if we had not kept moving every one of us would have died. We had known two years of war, but we came nearer to despair that night than I care to remember.*

After the Boer surrender in May 1902, Reitz left his homeland for Madagascar but was soon persuaded to return to the Transvaal by his former commander, Smuts. Ironically, during World War I (1914-1918), the onetime Boer commando fought with distinction for Britain against the Germans both in Africa and in France. After serving for many years in the Parliament and cabinet of the Union of South Africa, Reitz was appointed the Union's high commissioner to London in 1943.

* Quoted in Meredith, **Diamonds, Gold, and War**, pp. 457-458.

## BRITAIN'S WILLINGNESS TO NEGOTIATE

In April 1902, the British—with a 250,000-man army in South Africa that was more than 12 times the size of the Boer commando force—could easily have refused to enter into negotiations with Burger's peace delegation, holding out instead for a total military victory. Indeed, convinced that only an overwhelming triumph would allow Britain to remake postwar South Africa as High Commissioner Milner and other colonial officials saw fit, a clear-cut victory in the field was exactly what he wanted. There was just one acceptable way to conclude the conflict, he informed his staff, and that was "by winning it."[2] By early 1902, however, few other British leaders in England or in South Africa, including Commander in Chief Kitchener himself, shared Milner's belief that the empire must fight until its opponents were forced into an unconditional surrender.

Kitchener's willingness to negotiate with the enemy rather than hold out for a complete military victory mirrored the prevailing attitude within Britain's Conservative government in the spring of 1902. By this time, the war had lasted far longer, cost far more (approximately £220 million), and, owing to the commander in chief's callous policies toward Boer women and children, it had been more controversial than anyone in Britain could have foreseen in 1899. Spurred on by the public's growing discontent with the expensive and, in the view of many Britons, incompetently managed war, Salisbury and his cabinet, including Milner's old ally Colonial Secretary Chamberlain strongly favored ending the conflict sooner rather than later.

"The British public ran through a gamut of emotions" during the war's first year, observes author Smurthwaite. Among them were nationalistic indignation at the Boer's October ultimatum, pride as the expeditionary force departed England for South Africa, outrage over Black Week's humiliating defeats, and joy at the relief of Kimberley and Mafeking and collapse of Pretoria. Throughout the conflict's pre-guerilla phase, the small minority of Britons who openly opposed the war "were running against a tide of anti-Boer . . . jingoism that was constantly reinforced by the popular imperialism expressed by many organs of the press," Smurthwaite contends. Derisively and, for the most part, inaccurately labeled as "pro-Boers," those Britons who dared to question publicly the wisdom or morality of their nation's military venture in South Africa were "regarded as traitors and their meetings broken up amid considerable violence," he writes.[3] By the end of 1901, however, Emily Hobhouse's shocking account of conditions in the refugee camps, combined with concerns regarding the guerilla conflict's cost to the English taxpayer, had caused more and more Britons to become disillusioned with the war.

Aside from the rising public clamor at home, another factor propelling Kitchener toward negotiations with the Boers in 1902 was his conviction that a negotiated peace with the Boers would be more durable than a dictated one. Despite his brutal policies toward Boer civilians in the past, Kitchener believed it was in the British Empire's best interests to be magnanimous with the bitter-enders now that they were all but beaten. With the war winding down, Bill Nasson contends, Kitchener thought that lasting political stability in South Africa "could only be clinched through a fair measure of conciliation with the Boers, who had to be an accepted, indeed an essential, co-element of a reconstructed white settler order."[4]

## THE BOERS FLOAT A PEACE PLAN

On April 12, Burger and his delegation formally presented their plan for a "perpetual treaty of friendship and peace" to Kitchener at his stately headquarters in Melrose House in the heart of Pretoria.[5] Among other things, the peace proposal called for a mutual amnesty, bilingual public schools, and, most controversially, political independence for the two Boer republics. Although Kitchener realized full well that Salisbury and his cabinet would never agree to repeal Britain's annexation of the Orange Free State and Transvaal, he was eager for the talks to continue and therefore forwarded the delegation's terms to London.

To signal their eagerness to open talks with the Boer leadership, the Salisbury government quickly sent a peace blueprint of its own back to Pretoria. Although the proposal indicated a willingness to negotiate several of the Burger delegation's conditions, particularly amnesty, the Cabinet rejected the Boers' demand for political independence just as Kitchener had predicted. In response, Burger announced that his delegation would have to delay further negotiations until they had consulted with their commandos in the field regarding London's insistence that Boer political independence was not on the bargaining table.

Determined to keep the negotiations alive, Kitchener agreed to a series of local cease-fires in the Orange River and Transvaal colonies so that the Boer generals could meet with their scattered commando units. On May 15, having been promised safe passage by Kitchener, 60 elected representatives from the various commando groups traveled to the town of Vereeniging, 50 miles (80.5 km) south of Pretoria, to decide whether to proceed with the peace process, even at the price of renouncing their independence. Following several days of heated discussions, the delegates voted to send generals Smuts, Botha, de la Rey, de Wet, and Barry Hertzog to Pretoria with a compromise peace plan that would give the Boer republics at least some semblance of independence. The proposal called for certain parts of the Transvaal and Orange Free State to be administered as crown colonies, including the Witwatersrand region with its large uitlander population, and the remainder as British protectorates. (A colony is under the direct political control of another state, whereas a protectorate is typically a self-governing territory of a stronger, or "protector," state.)

From left, the Boer generals Koos de la Rey, Christiaan de Wet, and Louis Botha, as they looked in 1902, around the time of the signing of the Treaty of Vereeniging that ended the Boer War.

## AMNESTY, FINANCIAL AID, AND BLACK POLITICAL RIGHTS

When the Boer negotiating team formally presented their compromise plan to Kitchener and Milner in Pretoria on May 19, both men quickly rebuffed their proposal for allowing immediate self-rule in certain sections of the Transvaal and Orange River colonies. "Grant it," Kitchener declared, "and before a year is over we shall be at war again."[6] Nonetheless, despite his refusal to back down on the protectorate proposal, Kitchener was fully prepared to make significant concessions to the Boer delegation on a variety of other issues, most notably amnesty for Afrikaners who had taken up arms against the British in the Cape Colony as well as in the Boer republics, and to give financial assistance for Boers whose farms and livestock had been destroyed.

Regarding the issue of amnesty, Kitchener offered all Boer commandos a general pardon, with the exception of the estimated 10,000 Cape Afrikaners recruited by the Transvaal and Free State during the war to fight their British rulers. At first he insisted that all Cape rebels would face significant prison terms along with permanent disenfranchisement as punishment for turning against their government. During the course of the negotiations, however, Kitchener considerably softened his stance toward the Cape rebels, agreeing that only their top leaders would be thrown in jail. The financial terms Kitchener eventually approved for the draft treaty were also generous. The agreement pledged that Britain would pay £3 million— three times the amount originally offered—to help Boers in the Transvaal and Orange River colonies rebuild their ruined farms and homes.

After the draft treaty was sent to London for approval, Milner, convinced that Kitchener had given too much to the Boers, expected the document to be returned to Pretoria with extensive revisions. To the high commissioner's surprise, aside from some concerns regarding the wording of the financial clauses, the Cabinet's only major objection to the agreement centered on the issue of nonwhite voting rights. Throughout the negotiations, Kitchener had adamantly refused to give in to Boer demands to provide a definite timetable for establishing internal self-government in the Transvaal and Orange River colonies (something that the Cape Colony had been awarded in 1872 and Natal in 1893). At the prodding of Smuts and his team, however, he finally agreed to include a clause in the treaty deferring any discussion of voting rights for the colonies'

In order to negotiate a peace settlement, the British abandoned any efforts to ensure voting privileges for black Africans in South Africa. Seen here, a group shot of black Africans who worked with the Boers during the war.

nonwhite residents until after the former Boer territories were granted internal self-rule, whenever that might be. Given the Afrikaners' deep-seated conviction that God intended whites to rule over all other races, this arrangement meant that central South Africa's large black population was highly unlikely to receive the vote anytime in the foreseeable future.

The draft agreement's clause concerning nonwhite voting privileges put the Cabinet in an awkward position. From the conflict's outset, top British officials, including Prime Minister Salisbury and Colonial Secretary Chamberlain, had publicly identified securing greater rights for the Transvaal and Free State's oppressed black populations as one of Great Britain's war aims. Consequently, during ratification discussions, Chamberlain and others in the Cabinet argued strongly against allowing the clause to remain in the treaty. After Milner informed them that the Boers were threatening to withdraw from the peace negotiations if the clause was removed, however, the Cabinet caved in, figuring that the war-weary British public would not consider the protection of native rights an issue worth the delay of peace. The government's decision to sacrifice black political rights to the cause of ending the unpopular war as quickly as possible, Fremont-Barnes observes, "was to have major implications for the future of race relations in South Africa."[7]

## THE TREATY OF VEREENIGING

On May 28, 1902, the Cabinet returned the revised draft treaty to the assembled Boer delegates at Vereeniging. The Afrikaners were given just three days—until midnight on May 31—to accept or reject the document. Although the treaty was remarkably lenient toward the Boers on the issues of native voting rights, amnesty, and financial aid for reconstruction, the fact that it did not grant immediate self-government to the Transvaal and Orange River colonies was a major sticking point for some Boer leaders. Under Louis Botha's skillful direction, however, the peace faction within the Vereeniging delegation soon prevailed over bitter-enders such as General de Wet and President Steyn. During the ratification debates, Botha argued for approval on the grounds that neither the hungry and ill-supplied commandos in the field nor the thousands of homeless Boer women and children still on the veld could be expected to hold out much longer. When a vote on the treaty was taken on the afternoon of May 31, just hours before the deadline was due to expire, all but six of the 60 delegates gathered at Vereeniging voted for acceptance.

At 11:05 P.M. on May 31, 1902, Boer leaders formally signed what would come to be known as the Treaty of Vereeniging in the elegant dining room of Kitchener's headquarters at Melrose House. Botha and the other Boer generals had the difficult task of informing their troops that their nearly three-year struggle to preserve their independence was over. Rather than sign the required oath affirming their loyalty to King Edward VII (who succeeded his mother, Queen Victoria, to the British throne following her death in January 1901), some bitter-enders chose self-imposed exile in German Southwest Africa or Madagascar. Most, however, dejectedly signed the oath and returned home to their families and farms—or whatever was left of them. "To me," wrote Roland Schikkerling, a young commando from Johannesburg, after receiving the news of the surrender, "everything in which hope was, seems gone and I feel as if our liberty has been buried alive and our future stillborn. Our opportunities seem forever past and gone."[8]

# The Boer War's Aftermath

Although the Boer War officially ended in victory for Great Britain on May 31, 1902, the fact that its triumph over the much-smaller Boer force took nearly three years to accomplish did not reflect well on the British army. "The number of men, the amount of materiel, and the length of time required by mighty Britain to subdue a relative handful of South African farmers jolted Britain and amazed the world," Byron Farwell observes. "Among the many interested spectators to this revelation of Britain's limitations," he writes, "none perhaps was more interested than the Kaiser and the Great General Staff of the German army, which produced a detailed two-volume study of the conflict." It is impossible to know the extent to which the humiliating performance of the army, reputed to be one of the world's finest, influenced the militaristic Kaiser and his generals during the years immediately following the

Boer War. "But certainly they saw little to discourage their aggressive ambitions," contends Farwell, ambitions that would lead directly to the outbreak of World War I in August 1914, a dozen years after the Peace of Vereeniging.[1]

The imperial army's less-than-stellar showing against the Boer commandos produced widespread concern at home about Britain's ability to compete effectively against Germany and the other major European powers' larger and better-equipped forces. Consequently, beginning in 1902, the army inaugurated a series of reforms in administration, organization, training, and tactics "affecting the whole service. Regulars and part-timers alike, and from top to bottom," Barthorp writes.[2] The reforms ranged from the creation of an Imperial General Staff headed by the army's most senior-serving soldier to oversee the army's preparations for war, down to modifications in the personal equipment the soldiers carried and the uniforms they wore. From these sweeping reforms emerged the celebrated British Expeditionary Force (BEF). Deployed to France at the start of the First World War to repel the invading German army, the BEF was by far the best-trained, -equipped, and -organized fighting force to leave English shores up to that time. "The hard lessons" learned by the British army during their nearly three-year-long contest with the Boers, Smurthwaite contends, "would stand them in good stead as the Expeditionary Force took the field in France in 1914."[3]

## THE BOER WAR AND BLACK SOUTH AFRICANS

Kitchener's brutal wartime tactics left in their wake a devastated economy and landscape in South Africa. More than 50,000 Boer families whose farms had been razed filed claims for compensation in the weeks and months following the Peace of Vereeniging. Destitute black farmers and herders also looked to the new colonial administration headed by Alfred Milner (now officially governor of the Orange River and Transvaal colonies) for compensation for destroyed homes, livestock, and crops. Yet, despite the great damage inflicted on their property and livelihoods by Kitchener's scorched-earth policy, native African claimants received significantly less financial assistance from the British government than did their Boer counterparts. In the Transvaal, for example, London allocated more than £1 million to help reconstruct Boer-owned farms and resettle white concentration camp internees but only £16,000 to rebuild black-owned farms and resettle black refugees. "In several parts of the Transvaal, where the devastation had been particularly acute," Fremont-Barnes writes, "thousands of blacks continued to suffer from near-starvation even six months after the end

# BRITISH AUTHOR RUDYARD KIPLING AND THE BOER WAR

Five days after the governments of the Transvaal and Orange Free State declared war on Great Britain, popular British author and committed imperialist Rudyard Kipling composed a patriotic poem about the new conflict and the ordinary Britons who were being called upon to fight it. Entitled "The Absent-Minded Beggar," the poem was commissioned by a London newspaper to encourage public donations to its charitable fund for the dependents of the thousands of the soldiers ("gentlemen in khaki") who had been "ordered South" to save the empire from Paul Kruger and his Boer cronies. Kipling's patriotic verse is excerpted below:

> When you've shouted "Rule Britannia":
> When you've sung "God Save the Queen,"
> When you've finished killing Kruger with your mouth:
> Will you kindly drop a shilling in my little tambourine
> For a gentleman in khaki ordered South?
> He's an absent-minded beggar and his weaknesses are great:

of hostilities. With successive droughts worsening an already dreadful situation, many blacks had no choice but to become wage-earners working for white farmers where, before, they were landowners in their own right."[4]

Blacks who made their livings in the Rand's goldfields also found themselves worse off after the Peace of Vereeniging than before the war. Not only did the mines' notoriously bad working conditions decline even further under the new colonial regime, but to the disgust of the Rand's overwhelmingly black labor force, Milner refused to stand up for the miners when

---

But we and Paul must take him as we find him!
He is out on active service, wiping something off a slate:
And he's left a lot of little things behind him! . . .

Let us manage so as later we can look him in the face,
And tell him what he'd very much prefer:
That, while he saved the Empire, his employer saved his
    place,
And his mates (that's you and me) looked out for her.
He's an absent-minded beggar, and he may forget it all,
But we do not want his kiddies to remind him
That we sent 'em to the workhouse, while their daddy
    hammered Paul,
So we'll help the homes our Tommy's left behind him!

Cook's home—duke's home—home of a millionaire—
(Fifty thousand foot and horse going to Table Bay!)
Each of 'em doing his country's work (and what have you
    got to spare?)
Pass the hat for your credit's sake, and pay—pay—pay!*

---

* Rudyard Kipling, **The New World Edition of the Works of Rudyard Kipling**. Garden City, N.Y.: The Country Life Press, 1899, pp. 125,127.

profit-hungry owners slashed their monthly wages by nearly a third from prewar levels.

Black residents of the former Boer republics had good reason to resent their new overlords. During the Boer War, more than 100,000 blacks had provided invaluable assistance to the British army in a wide range of capacities, including as guards, messengers, drivers, and guides. Thousands of blacks died for the British cause between 1899 and 1902, including unknown numbers of native scouts and spies who were executed after being captured by Boer commandos. Yet any hopes Africans may have harbored that the British Empire would reward their loyalty and sacrifice were quickly dashed. Having long believed that Britain represented a more just and broad-minded political and social order, many blacks felt deeply betrayed when London, anxious to end the war as soon as possible, yielded to Boer demands to postpone any discussion of native voting rights until after the two colonies were self-governing.

## MILNER'S FAILED ANGLICIZATION PLAN

Neither the economic hardships nor the political oppression of postwar South Africa's black population were of much interest to the Transvaal and Orange River colonies' chief executive, Alfred Milner, who focused his attention instead on the long-dominant white minority. Determined to ensure continued British supremacy in the defeated Boer states, Milner wanted to transform the region into a "'thoroughly British' domain where 'British interests, British ideas, British education' would prevail."[5]

Milner planned to accomplish his ambitious goal of anglicizing (making English) the former Boer territories through two principal methods. First, he sought to encourage immediate and large-scale British immigration into the region. In five or six years, he optimistically expected, British-descended colonists would substantially outnumber Afrikaners, thereby all but guaranteeing that the onetime Boer states would remain within the imperial sphere, even if London decided to grant them internal self-government. Overhauling the colonies' educational system was the second way Milner intended to convert central South Africa into a "thoroughly British" domain. English was to replace Afrikaans as the principal medium of instruction in the public schools and the sole language of all higher education in the colonies, and teachers were to be carefully chosen for their loyalty to the imperial cause.

To Milner's immense frustration, his scheme to remake postwar central South Africa encountered serious obstacles from the start. Most significantly, British immigration to the region was far lower than anticipated, a problem Milner attributed to the colonies' stagnant postwar economies. Following the Peace of Vereeniging, serious labor shortages (brought on by the refusal of many black miners to work for reduced wages) plagued the gold mining industry, which had been the source of most of central South Africa's prewar wealth. Convinced that a revitalized economy would draw more British immigrants to the region, Milner decided to recruit thousands of indentured Chinese laborers to toil in the Rand's vast goldfields. The governor's policy of importing cheap Chinese labor into the Transvaal rapidly restored gold productivity in the colony to prewar levels. Yet, owing at least in part to the extremely negative publicity that it received at home, Milner's solution to the mining industry's labor shortage problem failed to boost British immigration to the annexed territories. Working for starvation wages and subjected to floggings by their white supervisors, the Chinese laborers were treated as little better than slaves—a situation that reflected poorly not only on South Africa's colonial administration but also on Great Britain. The governor's plan to promote British culture and suppress Afrikaner nationalism in the conquered territories by anglicizing their educational systems also ended up backfiring. Wider use of English in the schools, Judd and Surridge write, "did not relegate Afrikaans to the status of a second-class language," as he had hoped. "Indeed," they contend, "there is much evidence to show that Afrikaners, mocked at school and elsewhere as 'donkeys' if they refused to use English, reacted by clinging all the more determinedly to their language and sense of identity."[6]

## SOUTH AFRICA GAINS INTERNAL SELF-GOVENMENT

The first years after the Peace of Vereeniging witnessed a political as well as cultural revival among Afrikaners offended by Milner's heavy-handed policies. Several Boer political parties emerged during the period, including the popular Het Volk (People's) Party under former commando generals Louis Botha and Jan Smuts. While blasting Milner's leadership, Botha and Smuts also emphasized their willingness to work constructively with the British government to rebuild their homeland's shattered economy. Their conciliatory stance toward Britain paid off in 1906 when the Liberal Party, headed by one of the Boer War's fiercest critics in Parliament, Sir Henry Campbell-Bannerman, swept the Conservatives out of office.

After removing Milner from all his South African posts, Britain's new Liberal leadership granted internal self-government to the Transvaal and Orange River colonies. In the general elections of 1907, the two colonies' all white and predominantly Boer electorates voted in Afrikaner-dominated governments. To Smuts, Campbell-Bannerman's willingness to return political control of the former republics to Boer leaders just five years after the Peace of Vereeniging was "a miracle of trust and magnanimity." To Milner, on the other hand, it was "a great betrayal," both of the imperial cause and of the 22,000 British soldiers who had lost their lives during the Boer War.[7]

In 1910, at the strong urging of Botha and other Boer leaders, the British Parliament agreed to unite the Transvaal, Orange River, Natal, and Cape colonies as a self-governing dominion within the British Empire. That same year, Botha became the first prime minister of the new Union of South Africa. Botha and Smuts, who was elected prime minister after

Botha's untimely death in 1919, followed a policy of reconciliation toward Great Britain; South Africa even sent troops to fight alongside the British during World War I and World War II.

Still deeply embittered by the events of the Boer War, and particularly the loss of nearly 30,000 civilians in the British concentration camps, many Afrikaners scorned Botha and Smuts's approach toward London. In 1914, a group of Afrikaner nationalists committed to total separation from the empire founded their own political organization, the National Party. While the Nationalists' political fortunes rose and fell over the next three decades, they were in firm control of the South African government by 1948. Almost immediately, they began to work toward two major goals. The first of these was ensuring continued white political and economic domination over the country's ever-growing nonwhite population under the notorious apartheid (Afrikaans for "separateness") system. The Nationalists' second main goal, achieving total independence from Britain, was finally realized in 1961 when the British government allowed South Africa to become an independant republic.

## APARTHEID AND ITS BOER WAR ROOTS

From the earliest years of the Union, South Africa's black majority had been subjected to a barrage of oppressive legislation, including the 1913 Natives' Land Act, which prohibited them from buying or renting the more than 90 percent of the country's land that lay outside of specially designated "native reserves." Once the stridently racist National Party came to power, the blacks' situation only worsened as the Nationalists quickly expanded the Union's already repressive racial policies to create "the most elaborate racial edifice the world has ever seen—a vast apparatus of laws and controls to enforce white supremacy." Under the Nationalists' tyrannical apartheid program, Martin Meredith writes, "every facet of [native] African life—residence, employment, education, public amenities and politics—was regulated to ensure their subordination."[8]

Jan Christian Smuts served as prime minister of South Africa twice. Although he supported racial segregation, his government issued the 1948 Fagan Report, which stated that complete segregation was impractical. That same year, his party narrowly lost the general election to the National Party, which created the formal system of apartheid.

Although apartheid was first instituted in South Africa nearly a half century after the Peace of Vereeniging, many historians see a direct connection between its development and the Boer War. They argue that the destructive conflict only served to harden traditional Boer attitudes regarding their special status as a chosen people and the threat that their supposedly inferior black neighbors posed to them. The Afrikaners believed that God had severely tested them during the war. Yet within a decade, the Afrikaners were once again in charge of their own domestic affairs and had even expanded their influence in southern Africa under the auspices of the newly created Union of South Africa: clear evidence, many Afrikaners asserted, of God's special favor toward them.

The Afrikaners' wartime experiences also reinforced a long-standing Boer assumption that was at the heart of apartheid philosophy: the success of their divine mission—indeed, their very survival—in South Africa depended upon their ability to control its vast "heathen" population. Although black South Africans "behaved with unexpected restraint" toward their Boer oppressors throughout most of the war, Thomas Pakenham observes, a rash of Boer raids on native villages prompted several tribal groups to launch deadly retaliatory attacks on local commando units during the conflict's final months.[9] Alarmed by what appeared to be a new spirit of militancy among South Africa's indigenous peoples, many Afrikaners entered the postwar era more wary than ever of the region's downtrodden black majority.

## THE BOER WAR'S "WORST LEGACY"

In 1902, eager to end the unpopular war as quickly as possible, the British government caved in to Afrikaner demands that all discussion of black voting rights in the fallen republics be postponed until after they became self-governing, in what Pakenham calls the Boer War's "worst legacy." In 1910, when the Union of South Africa was formed, the British government once again

Following the collapse of the apartheid system, the inauguration of Nelson Mandela in 1994 as South Africa's first black
president was seen as a watershed moment in the history of
the nation. Mandela is seen here at center, raising F.W. de Klerk's
(*left*) and Thabo Mbeki's hands in triumph.

disregarded native political rights. To encourage postwar unity among British- and Dutch-descended whites, and, Pakenham asserts, "because of a guilty conscience toward Afrikaners" stemming from Lord Kitchener's harsh policies toward Boer civilians, London permitted Afrikaner leaders to permanently bar the Union's nonwhite residents from voting in three out of its four provinces.[10] Only in the Cape were native Africans, assuming they could meet stringent financial qualifications, granted the vote, a privilege they lost in 1934 when all blacks were summarily removed from the province's common roll. (All other nonwhite voters, including Asians and mixed-race South Africans, were eliminated from the Cape's common roll in 1948.)

South Africa's white Afrikaner leadership continued to tightly control the country's political and economic affairs and repress the rights of its large black majority throughout most of the twentieth century. As the century wore on, however, this unbridled white power came under growing attack both from the black nationalists and from many members of the international community, who sought to force an end to South Africa's racist policies by imposing economic sanctions on the country. Finally, after decades of petitions, protest marches, and strikes by the nation's increasingly militant black majority, the South African Parliament passed legislation in 1993 that guaranteed equal voting rights, regardless of race. One year later, the country's first-ever free elections resulted in an overwhelming victory for the anti-apartheid and pro-democracy African National Congress (ANC) party. The charismatic and highly respected head of the ANC, Nelson Mandela—who had been imprisoned by the Nationalist government for nearly 30 years for his anti-apartheid activities—became South Africa's first black president. Today, following almost two decades of multiracial democratic rule in South Africa, the Boer War's most lasting and most reviled legacy—apartheid—is nothing more than a bitter memory.

# CHRONOLOGY

| | |
|---|---|
| 1652 | Dutch East India Company founds the Cape of Good Hope settlement. |
| 1815 | Britain officially annexes Cape Colony following end of the Napoleonic Wars. |
| 1833 | British Parliament abolishes slavery throughout the British Empire. |
| 1834 | Great Trek of the Boers out of Cape Colony begins. |
| 1843 | Boer coastal republic of Natal is annexed by Britain. |
| 1852 | Britain recognizes independence of the Transvaal. |

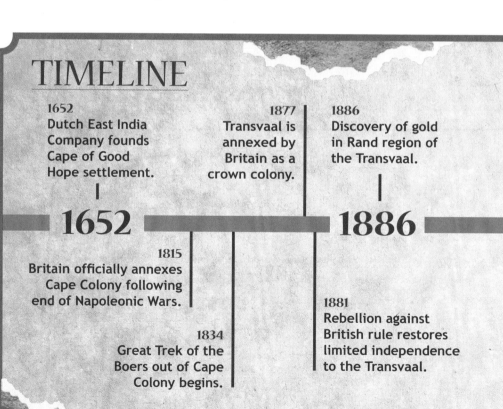

## TIMELINE

**1652**
Dutch East India Company founds Cape of Good Hope settlement.

**1877**
Transvaal is annexed by Britain as a crown colony.

**1886**
Discovery of gold in Rand region of the Transvaal.

**1652**

**1886**

**1815**
Britain officially annexes Cape Colony following end of Napoleonic Wars.

**1834**
Great Trek of the Boers out of Cape Colony begins.

**1881**
Rebellion against British rule restores limited independence to the Transvaal.

1854    Britain recognizes independence of the Orange Free State.

1871    Diamond-rich Kimberley region is annexed to Cape Colony.

1877    Transvaal is annexed by Britain as a crown colony.

1879    Britain defeats Zulu kingdom in the Anglo-Zulu War.

1881    Rebellion against British rule restores limited independence to the Transvaal.

1886    Discovery of gold in Rand region of the Transvaal.

1895    Joseph Chamberlain is appointed British Colonial Secretary.

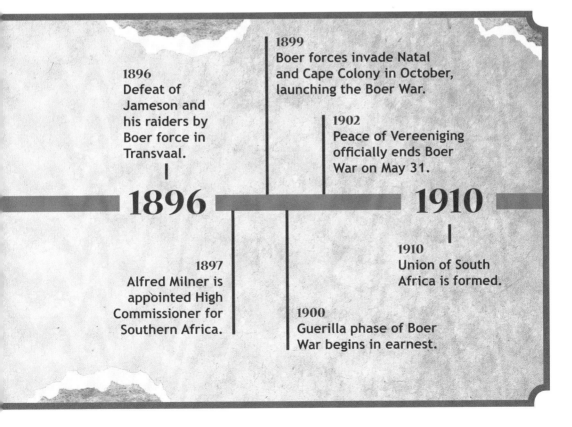

1896
Defeat of Jameson and his raiders by Boer force in Transvaal.

1899
Boer forces invade Natal and Cape Colony in October, launching the Boer War.

1902
Peace of Vereeniging officially ends Boer War on May 31.

**1896**

**1910**

1897
Alfred Milner is appointed High Commissioner for Southern Africa.

1900
Guerilla phase of Boer War begins in earnest.

1910
Union of South Africa is formed.

| | |
|---|---|
| **1896** | Defeat of Jameson and his raiders by Boer force in the Transvaal. |
| **1896** | The Transvaal and the Orange Free State form defensive military alliance. |
| **1897** | Alfred Milner is appointed High Commissioner for Southern Africa. |
| **1899** | Boer forces invade Natal and Cape Colony in October, launching the Boer War. |
| **1900** | Orange Free State capital of Bloemfontein falls to British; Transvaal capital of Pretoria falls to British; guerilla phase of Boer War begins in earnest. |
| **1902** | Peace of Vereeniging officially ends Boer War on May 31. |
| **1910** | Union of South Africa is formed. |

# NOTES

## CHAPTER 2

1. David Smurthwaite, *The Boer War: 1899–1902*. London: Hamlyn, 1999, p. 14.
2. Gregory Fremont-Barnes, *The Boer War: 1899–1902*. Oxford: Osprey Publishing, 2003, p. 13.
3. Quoted in Denis Judd and Keith Surridge, *The Boer War*. New York: Palgrave MacMillan, 2002, p. 21.
4. Thomas Pakenham, *The Boer War*. New York: Random House, 1979, p. 9.
5. Smurthwaite, *The Boer War*, p. 15.
6. Bill Nasson, *The South African War: 1899–1902*. London: Arnold, 1999, p. 4.
7. Fremont-Barnes, *The Boer War*, p. 14.
8. Pakenham, *The Boer War*, p. 11.
9. Ibid.
10. Quoted in Martin Meredith, *Diamonds, Gold, and War: The British, the Boers, and the Making of South Africa*. New York: Public Affairs, 2007, p. 98.

## CHAPTER 3

1. Michael Barthorp, *Slogging Over Africa: The Boer Wars 1815–1902*. London: Cassell, 1987, p. 43.
2. Ibid.
3. Quoted in Meredith, *Diamonds, Gold, and War*, p. 104.

4. Fremont-Barnes, *The Boer War*, p. 19.
5. Brian Roberts, *Those Bloody Women: Three Heroines of the Boer War*. London: John Murray, 1991, p. 10.
6. Quoted in Meredith, *Diamonds, Gold, and War*, p. 156.
7. Barthorp, *Slogging Over Africa*, p. 47.
8. Ibid.
9. Quoted in Pakenham, *The Boer War*, p. 27.
10. Fremont-Barnes, *The Boer War*, p. 30.
11. Byron Farwell, *The Great Anglo-Boer War*. New York: Harper & Row, 1976, p. 33.
12. Quoted in Roberts, *Those Bloody Women*, p. 13.

## CHAPTER 4

1. Quoted in Pakenham, *The Boer War*, p. 54.
2. Quoted in Farwell, *The Great Anglo-Boer War*, p. 35.
3. Quoted in Meredith, *Diamonds, Gold, and War*, p. 414.
4. Quoted in Barthorp, *Slogging Over Africa*, p. 48.
5. Quoted in Nasson, *The South African War*, p. xiii.
6. Quoted in Meredith, *Diamonds, Gold, and War*, p. 422.
7. Ibid., pp. 422–423.
8. Quoted in Roberts, *Those Bloody Women*, p. 14.

9. Fremont-Barnes, *The Boer War*, p. 47.

10. Meredith, *Diamonds, Gold, and War*, p. 433.

11. Quoted in Fremont-Barnes, *The Boer War*, p. 47.

## CHAPTER 5

1. Quoted in Fremont-Barnes, *The Boer War*, p. 57.

2. Fremont-Barnes, *The Boer War*, p. 57.

3. Smurthwaite, *The Boer War*, p. 114.

4. Ibid., p. 56.

5. Pakenham, *The Boer War*, p. 408.

6. Meredith, *Diamonds, Gold, and War*, p. 442.

## CHAPTER 6

1. Meredith, *Diamonds, Gold, and War*, p. 449.

2. Smurthwaite, *The Boer War*, p. 136.

3. Nasson, *The South African War*, p. 212.

4. Fremont-Barnes, *The Boer War*, p. 63.

5. Quoted in Meredith, *Diamonds, Gold, and War*, p. 451.

6. Ibid.

7. Quoted in Nasson, *The South African War*, p. 220.

8. Farwell, *The Great Anglo-Boer War*, p. 393.

9. Ibid., p. 392.

10. Quoted in Meredith, *Diamonds, Gold, and War*, p. 455.

11. Ibid., pp. 456–457.

12. Pakenham, *The Boer War*, p. 548.

## CHAPTER 7

1. Quoted in Meredith, *Diamonds, Gold, and War*, p. 459.

2. Quoted in Pakenham, *The Boer War*, p. 584.

3. Smurthwaite, *The Boer War*, p. 158.

4. Nasson, *The South African War*, p. 231.

5. Quoted in Pakenham, *The Boer War*, p. 585.

6. Quoted in Meredith, *Diamonds, Gold, and War*, p. 465.

7. Fremont-Barnes, *The Boer War*, p. 84.

8. Quoted in Judd and Surridge, *The Boer War*, p. 296.

## CHAPTER 8

1. Farwell, *The Great Anglo-Boer War*, p. xii.

2. Barthorp, *Slogging Over Africa*, p. 164.

3. Smurthwaite, *The Boer War*, p. 193.

4. Fremont-Barnes, *The Boer War*, p. 88.

5. Quoted in Meredith, *Diamonds, Gold, and War*, p. 482.

6. Judd and Surridge, *The Boer War*, p. 299.

7. Quoted in Meredith, *Diamonds, Gold, and War*, p. 493.

8. Ibid., p. 525.

9. Pakenham, *The Boer War*, p. 601.

10. Ibid., p. 612.

# BIBLIOGRAPHY

Barthorp, Michael. *Slogging Over Africa: The Boer Wars, 1815–1902*. London: Cassell, 1987.

Evans, Martin Marix. *The Boer War: South Africa 1899–1902*. Oxford: Osprey Publishing, 1999.

Farwell, Byron. *The Great Anglo-Boer War*. New York: Harper & Row, 1976.

Fremont-Barnes, Gregory. *The Boer War: 1899–1902*. Oxford: Osprey Publishing, 2003.

Grundlingh, Albert. "The Bitter Legacy of the Boer War." *History Today*, November 1999, pp. 21–25.

Judd, Denis, and Keith Surridge. *The Boer War*. New York: Palgrave MacMillan, 2002.

LaBand, John, ed. *Daily Lives of Civilians in Wartime Africa: From Slavery Days to Rwandan Genocide*. Westport, Conn.: Greenwood Press, 2007.

Meredith, Martin. *Diamonds, Gold, and War: The British, the Boers, and the Making of South Africa*. New York: Public Affairs, 2007.

Nasson, Bill. *The South African War: 1899–1902*. London: Arnold, 1999.

Pakenham, Thomas. *The Boer War*. New York: Random House, 1979.

Roberts, Brian. *Those Bloody Women: Three Heroines of the Boer War*. London: John Murray, 1991.

Smurthwaite, David. *The Boer War: 1899–1902*. London: Hamlyn, 1999.

Warwick, Peter. *Black People and the South African War: 1899–1902*. Cambridge: Cambridge University Press, 1983.

# FURTHER RESOURCES

## BOOKS

Corona, Laurel. *South Africa*. San Diego: Lucent Books, 2000.

Evans, Martin Marix. *Encyclopedia of the Boer War, 1899–1902*. Santa Barbara: ABC-CLIO, 2000.

Fish, Bruce, and Becky Durost Fish. *South Africa: 1880 to the Present: Imperialism, Nationalism, and Apartheid*. Philadelphia: Chelsea House, 2000.

Knight, Ian, and Gerry Embleton. *The Boer Wars, 1898–1902*. London: Osprey, 1997.

## WEB SITES

The Anglo-Boer War
   http://www.angloboerwar.com/

Anglo-Boer War Museum
   http://www.anglo-boer.co.za/

Perspectives: The South African War: Original and Contemporary Sources
   http://www.pinetreeweb.com/perspectives.htm

South Africa.Info: A Short History of South Africa
   http://www.southafrica.info/about/history/history.htm

# PICTURE CREDITS

119

# INDEX

# ABOUT THE AUTHOR

**LOUISE CHIPLEY SLAVICEK** received her master's degree in history from the University of Connecticut. She is the author of numerous articles on American and world history for scholarly journals and young people's magazines, including *Cobblestone* and *Calliope*. Her more than 30 books for young people include *Women of the American Revolution, Israel, Daniel Inouye, The San Francisco Earthquake and Fire of 1906, The Chinese Cultural Revolution*, and *Paul Robeson*.